Reviews fo[illegible]

Nikki has written not only an inspiring [illegible] how to transform your life, but also a practical and information rich guide to house sitting. This is a must read for anyone searching for a bit of adventure in their lives and who would like to try house sitting as a way to travel on a budget!

Kylie Fuad
Director
www.AussieHouseSitters.com.au

Nikki Ah Wong gets it! Her book demonstrates, once again, that living life on our own terms is the best way to find the satisfaction that we all seek. House sitting is one way to support a dream. Whatever your dream might be, when people like Nikki tell their personal stories of triumph, it empowers us all.

Teresa Roberts author of "Finding the Gypsy in Me -Tales of an International House Sitter"
www.findingthegypsyinme.com

Housesitting In Australia

Big adventures on a tiny budget

Nikki Ah Wong

Although this is a work of non-fiction, some names have been changed to protect the privacy of the families involved.

ISBN-13: 978-0-9872553-0-3
ISBN-10: 0987255304

Dedication

This book is dedicated to my big wonderful
family. To my sons, grandchildren,
and nieces and nephews,
may you discover your passion early
and find your own adventures.

Contents

Preface

When I started writing, I never envisaged my stories turning into a book. I just wanted to document all the wonderful adventures I was having.

I kept notes and took photos and then one day I realised that I really did have a story to tell.

This is not just a story about my travels and adventures, but also the story of how I got to where I am today. This is a story of hope and maybe just a little courage.

When times were tough, I looked ahead and set goals and went with what was in my heart. It worked for me.

It is also about housesitting.

Many people have asked me how I got into housesitting. Others want to know if it could work for them. Maybe it could.

Housesitting gave me a lifestyle that many people dream of, and I didn't need to be rich to get it.

This year I have learned so much about myself and about what makes me happy. I learned about love, and life, and about making your own fun. This is my story and I hope it might inspire you so try something new for yourself. It might be housesitting, or it might be Hang gliding. It could be writing your own story or maybe running a marathon.

If my story helps at least one person begin a life of passion and adventure then I will be happy.

I hope you can be that person.

May all your dreams come true.

Acknowledgements

This has been the most amazing year. I have been living a dream and I have so many people to thank for their support during this time.

While I have been following my heart and my dreams, I have not been able to contribute financially to my student sons, visit my boys as often as I would have liked, or offer anything but the most modest birthday and other gifts. The question "What does your mother do?" must have been as difficult for them as it was for me. I would like to thank my sons for their understanding and patience.

My ex-husband has been forging his new life too and I would like to thank him for supporting our sons during this time both financially and in person, and for making it possible for me spend time with them, especially the youngest.

I wish to thank the families who trusted me with the care of their homes and their wonderful pets. Each of your homes was different and interesting and you made my stay very comfortable.

Finally and most importantly, I would like to thank Phil. He has been my rock and his support has been crucial to both the wonderful life I have lived this year, and the fact that I have had time and resources to write about it. Without him, there would have been no yellow bike, no year of wonder, and no book.

With all my heart, I love you Phil. I wish everyone had someone as wonderful as you in their life. Thank you so much for everything.

May our adventures continue forever.

Best Wishes - *Nikki*

Security is mostly a superstition. It does not exist in nature, nor do the children of men as a whole experience it. Avoiding danger is no safer in the long run than outright exposure. Life is either a daring adventure, or nothing.

(Helen Keller)

Prologue - The Dream

The sand on this beach looks like raw sugar mingled with white sugar and laced with honey coloured flecks and the odd miniscule stone chip or shell fragment.

Running my hands through it reminds me of Japanese raked gardens. I make curved line patterns in the sand with my fingers as I watch the sun set, in a blaze of gold over the mangrove trees on the mainland shore.

I am in paradise. My body glows inside and out. The sun is just the width of my hand up in the sky and still warm and soothing. It feels nice on my skin and I am enjoying topping up my fading Queensland tan.

This morning I went scuba diving. The diving instructor was kind. He didn't laugh when I said I had a prehistoric diving license I had not used since 1970. Then he assessed me as needing a women's regular sized suit. It was like trying to stuff 20 kilos of bread dough into a 10-kilo black rubber pouch. I had to return it for one two sizes bigger but I was immensely flattered.

Within meters of the shore, and less than three meters down, my ears began to hurt badly. I danced, I hovered, and I floated up and down holding my nose and puffing madly. I pictured the air bubbles exploding in the canals of my ears and worried about permanent damage.

Finally, the pain subsided and we started down into a stunning world of colourful coral and remarkable sea life.

The coral fingered and clumped into lunar like patterns in subdued purples and neon orange. There was a spiny, spiky, puffed up stonefish, and several little stingrays that whirled off quickly, leathery wings swaying gracefully.

My instructor pointed out a sea hare, looking like two huge fans hiding a little stem between the large brown leaves, and little black plants that curled in their leafy fronds as we touched them.

A small turtle swam cautiously by, along with a little orange boxfish that looked like it had been blown full of air. A blind shark lay still on the seabed, playing dead in the water.

Suddenly a huge blue sideways flying saucer of a fish appeared heading straight for me. He had a fearsome looking droopy lower jaw with dangly looking teeth that looked like he had lost a fight with a pit bull. At twenty centimetres he was larger than a flattened basketball, bulbous, bright blue, and scarily intimidating. He swam up close. I held my breath.

Taking my cue from my dive instructor, I stayed calm and gingerly put out my hand to touch him. He circled me and swam off lazily.

This is Nelsons Bay, a marine park on the central coast of New South Wales, Australia, and this is typical of my life now. Could it be any better?

While my previous workmates are heading off to offices in their air-conditioned high-rises, I am often outside enjoying myself. I could be setting up a web page about 5 minute chocolate mug cakes, or maybe exploring a beautiful Aussie Park looking for hidden treasure. I write, I explore, and I learn. Most of all I have fun and an enormous amount of free time.

In the last year, I have lived on an organic health farm, and a hobby farm; in a recently constructed urban ghetto development, a Midwest country town, and several up market homes in inner city Brisbane. I have spent the night in a luxury Brisbane high-rise overlooking the city, and in a shabby pub room that another tenant described as, "like staying in the back of a stock truck."

I have started riding a beautiful old yellow Honda 250cc motorbike and have done over eight thousand kilometres, even though it has been off the road many times for repairs. I have taken it around lower east Queensland and through to the western slopes of New South Wales. I have taken it down to Melbourne and across Tasmania; not bad for a fifty-year-old grandmother.

I do what I enjoy and I love it. It amazes me when I think about how my life has changed in the last year. I am living proof that age is no barrier to changing your life for the better. In this book, I will show you how I managed on a small amount of money each week, while having the time of my life.

Maybe you could too. You can become a motorbike riding Granny or a perpetual explorer or something completely different. Where do you want to be in a year from now? Plan it, dream it, and do it. I hope this book inspires you and gives you some ideas to increase the joy in your own life.

My life is amazing now, and it is all thanks to the magic of housesitting; the job that is not really a job.

The Road to Housesitting

I didn't plan to be a house sitter. I didn't even intend to go to Australia.

I went to New Zealand as a young child and always felt lucky to be there. Over the years, I watched amazed as thousands of New Zealanders including many family and friends, moved across the ditch to Australia.

I thought they were unpatriotic to leave such a beautiful country like ours. I loved New Zealand, and assumed it would always be home. Then, an extraordinary series of events changed my life dramatically.

***

I sat in front of my family doctor and tried to find a way to tell him I was depressed again. This was my third visit in a month, because on the first two visits I had not been able to bring myself to confess my real reason for coming. We discussed my thyroid problems, my suspected gallstones, and possible infections.

Finally, I blurted out that I needed Prozac again.

It was ten years since he had first diagnosed me with depression and I had recognised it only once since then. Each time, I took one week of Prozac and felt better.

Normally a happy person, I had been feeling the same helplessness and unfocussed overwhelming sadness that I had before. The days seemed to close in on themselves. I was unable to picture anything past the end of the day or to plan ahead. When I started sobbing at the shopping centre because a mother had a noisy child she could not control, I knew I needed help again.

This time the doctor looked me in the eye and told me firmly that I would have to take anti-depressants for the rest of my life. He gave me a three months' supply of Prozac and strict instructions not to stop taking it without talking to him.

I took it for just one week and began to study natural methods of depression cures.

I took lots of walks, got as much sunshine as I could in the gloomy Wellington climate, and lost some weight. I even got a job. I loved the challenge and the people I worked with. I loved that people were paying me for things I used to do free in voluntary roles, and it was a big boost to my self-esteem. I no longer had depression but I was still unhappy.

I looked further for answers. I was unhappiest at home. My marriage was lifeless and my six sons were becoming adults and starting to drift into their own lives.

I was sometimes incredibly lonely. I would often cook a meal and then eat alone as they all did their own thing. The lowest point was when I stopped cooking altogether and no one seemed to mind.

The day I read a study about how children laugh more than adults do, I had a light bulb moment. I did not laugh even once a day and could not remember whether I had laughed at all in the last few years. I began to study happy people, and one in particular who made even me laugh. I met his family and they all had fun. I wanted that.

I spent several years weighing up the heavy stone of

guilt at breaking up a family, against the bright feathers that could be my happiness and decided I would stay for sake of my boys.

One day I finally realised that my boys didn't need an unhappy and sullen parent.

I approached my husband and asked what he thought I could do to improve our marriage. He flicked his eyes at me for only a few minutes and replied, "There is nothing" before returning to what he was doing. Two weeks later, I finally had the courage to leave my husband and move out on my own.

***

Six months later, I sat in my cramped one bedroom flat with my fingers poised over the computer keyboard and began to dream. I had read a book called "The Secret" and I knew all about the laws of attraction. I was prepared to ask the universe for everything I might possibly need for a wonderful life.

"I have a wonderful relationship with a man that I love and respect. He honours and adores me," I wrote and mentally underlined.

"I have a wonderful relationship with my boys and we enjoy time together often," I typed. The boys still lived at home and I did not see them as often as I would have liked. I missed them.

"I live in a beautiful home next to beautiful parks and close to the ocean."

I wanted it all. I asked the universe to send me money, adventures, good health, and travel, lots of travel.

I spent hours choosing fonts and graphics and illustrating it lavishly with photos of my boys, pictures of money and dazzlingly beautiful vistas of tropical beaches and exotic villages in faraway places. For many mornings, I would read it and dream.

Two years later, everything on my list has come true except for one, perhaps the most surprising one of all. I have everything I have ever wanted and more but I have very little money, perhaps less than I did when I wrote the list, but I am happy; so very, very, happy.

Life is good but it had to get worse before it got better.

***

Six months after I wrote my list, I was in my eleventh floor office overlooking Porirua City. It was a sunny Friday afternoon in the middle of a cool Wellington winter and I was looking out the window. As the only high rise in the region, the views were spectacular. Like a Richard Scary tiny town, everything in the city below seemed to be visible from here.

Cars wove in and out along the little grey strips that were streets and little people dots rushed back and forth. A silver ribbon of river divided the city buildings from the railway and behind that, the tiny houses backed by the mounds of green that made up the suburb of Cannons Creek. By leaning out, I could see where the river flowed across large washes of mud flats into the sparkling blue harbour.

I was quietly getting on with some paperwork and looking forward to going home in a few hours when, unexpectedly, the Regional Manager appeared at my office door and asked me to follow her to her office. She looked miserable and my mind went through a few possible scenarios. We were responsible for nine childcare centres in the Wellington region and two further afield. I wondered what the tragedy was. With my boss away, I assumed that as the next level manager I was going to have to deal with it.

In my previous role, two of the teachers I managed had attracted international media attention by taking seven pre-schoolers on a walk through a motorway tunnel. I had handled redundancies, fired misbehaving cleaners, and supported a centre after one of the teachers died of a mystery illness.

I knew I was experienced and would cope with whatever was happening, but the Regional Manager continued to look miserable as she led me to her office and it seemed to be directed at me.

It was not what I expected.

After a brief reminder of the national recession and with what sounded like real regret, she explained that my position was to be made redundant. In my own professional and dignified way, I broke into tears and was unable to say anything much at all.

I spent the weekend considering my options.

I am usually an optimistic person. Although it hurt to be discarded as if I was an unwanted old sock, I decided to make the best of it. I believe that everything happens for a reason and we have the experiences we are supposed to have. I decided to look for the silver lining.

By Monday morning, I was feeling much more positive. I had been considering moving to Australia and this was going to make it happen.

I had several reasons to want to go to Australia.

Firstly, although I had left my ex-husband the family home so he could continue his home-based business, he had moved to Australia with the youngest who at almost twelve years old was the only one under eighteen. I would love to be able to see more of my youngest son.

Secondly, I had met a wonderful Australian man online.

Phil had also recently broken up from a long-term marriage. He had been living in New Zealand's cold south and working in a gold mine when I met him, but had since moved back to Australia.

At first, his emails were friendly but unremarkable, but they soon became the highlight of my day. I learned about his adventures in Antarctica, his scuba dive courses and his job. His emails were funny, interesting and sometimes illustrated by little computer drawn images of a cartoon man with a lopsided head.

By the time he began calling and texting me I knew I was going to like him. By the time I left New Zealand, I was in love.

On our first date, Phil had received a call from the police on his cell phone. They asked if I was with him and if I was okay. He came to my room looking amused.

He said that Josh had reported me missing and in possible danger. The police didn't seem to be too worried and were easily reassured. I have a feeling they had heard from Josh before.

I met Josh online around the same time I met Phil. He was a house-bound alcoholic who also had other serious addictions. I had never met him, and never planned to, but I had spoken to him many times. He said he was concerned for my safety. I suspect he just wanted to cause trouble.

Phil thought it was hilarious and spent the rest of our time together pretending to run out of petrol on remote windy roads and suggesting he had an axe in the boot.

When I got back to work, Josh's bitterness got worse. He sent a letter to the CEO of my organisation, accusing me of all sorts of crimes, from misuse of the company car, to abusing the children.

My managers had to take the accusation seriously and interviewed me several times. They were not sympathetic and I was mortified. They needed to show they had done something so they gave me a warning for driving a few hundred metres out of my way in the company car.

I had used my own car for work many times, so when I put in my claim, the organisation ended up owing me money, but the warning stood.

I concluded that the warning was probably a factor in my redundancy and so in a way, Josh got his wish to disrupt my life. I lost my job along with my company car, phone, and laptop.

Six weeks later, I left New Zealand with a new man and a new adventurous attitude to life, but I would have been very surprised had I known that a year later I would have become a sort of motorbike-riding gypsy that looks after other peoples home for a living.

The Retreat

My first situation was not a house sit but a room at a health retreat. I arrived during a promotional presentation. Ten retreat employees were explaining centre philosophy to just four visitors. It had all the religious fervour of an Amway presentation.

The retreat catered for people with anxiety, depression, and substance addictions using a regime of life coaching, pampering, organic food, and exercise.

The guests stayed in small cabins in amongst the avocado trees laden with ripening and fallen fruit, and came to the retreat for therapies and meals. At the gate was a large lake where I sometimes spent the early mornings watching platypus, turtles, and water dragons.

Clients paid more than my previous monthly salary to stay here. Some of the exclusive guests paid four times as much.

I met rich Americans, Canadians, and a smattering of Australians including the owner of a resort island in the Whitsundays.

At first, I lived in a room at the retreat but later I moved into a luxury home to "supervise" a recovering alcoholic in the evenings. This was a surprising twist of fate after my experiences with Josh, the bitter alcoholic.

I met some amazing people who had come to the retreat to try to improve their lives and each had an interesting story.

At five am one morning, I sat with a new arrival as

he told me about some spiritual experiences he had after his baby daughter died. Another client had lost a young son. They found solace with each other.

Most were recovering alcoholics or drug addicts but some were there to try to stop smoking or to deal with food issues.

One woman would eat nothing but raw baby spinach and sat apart during meals with a bowl of the greens on her lap.

Another guest also ate alone. She had her meals delivered to the private villa where she stayed so no one else would see her as she ate. She ate nothing during the day and ploughed through four enormous platters of specially prepared chicken, salad and steamed vegetables at night. After her two-week stay, she was able to eat an apple for lunch.

Both women were painfully thin and weak. I was often worried that their hearts would just stop beating right in front of me.

I was keen to be able to help, so I attended the group meetings along with the clients and then trained at the retreat as a life coach. The focus of their therapy was on self-acceptance. Clients were encouraged to see life as a journey and themselves as being in the only place they could be, given their past.

This was immensely reassuring to many of the people there who had made some bad choices in life, and they seemed to respond well. I prefer to see myself as having some choice about what happens to me and I am a convert to the power of good goals. I liked the concept but I didn't see it as that simple, or that helpful to clients.

While clients seemed to respond well during their stay, I wondered how much of that was just because they were away from society, and separated from their drug of choice. I later learned of several people who committed suicide after returning home from the retreat.

Along with client care, I did everything from weeding the garden and washing the car to removing cobwebs off the buildings. I even took publicity photos of one of the homes and designed web pages for their new depression program.

I enjoyed these jobs better than weeding, but I began to feel exploited. I only received an allowance of one hundred dollars a week, and that was always paid late. There are not many web designers working for that kind of money.

Before I left New Zealand, I had applied for an assistant manager role but I was never interviewed and no one was appointed. Within weeks of my arrival, I began to suspect it was only advertised to get people like myself to come and work while they waited.

A young couple arrived to head the fitness department and an Asian doctor from New Zealand said she had come to do beauty therapy. A health club manager from New Zealand said she had applied for the same job I had. They all arrived full of enthusiasm, worked for up to a week, and then left disillusioned.

I stayed three long months.

Friends that worked in the office started to disappear. They were at their desk one day and gone the next. Sometimes we were told it was a sudden layoff to cut costs. Other times, colleagues did not know why they had left. People who had paid jobs must have spent each day wondering when the axe would fall on them.

Then the retreat manager told me that the owner was giving her a brand new BMW for Christmas. Two days later the owner told everyone else that the centre was not making money and needed to cut costs again.

This was not how I wanted to live my life.

Most of my previous roles were voluntary. I chose them because I believed in a cause and enjoyed working with people who had strong values of charity, compassion, empathy, and kindness.

I suspect I am a little naïve. I left both my recent paid jobs because I did not want to work for people who were dishonest and treated people badly. On the other hand, I have always moved on to something better and my life now is awesome. I am glad for the experience but also that I did not accept that things have to be that way. Life can be so good.

I am a big believer in letting failure lead you to success, in learning from the past, and in always moving forward.

Whoever wrote the immortal lines "when God closes a door, he opens a window," was not telling the whole story. Sometimes he opens up a whole world of options.

For me, divorce, redundancy, and failure in my first role in Australia, were the catalysts I needed to look at an unusual option I had only heard about.

I applied for a housesitting role.

Other People's Homes

I was very lucky to get my first housesitting job.

I had no experience, no references and I turned up for the interview on a noisy motorbike, and wearing a bikie jacket that was not quite clean of dust and bug entrails. The owner was very kind and agreed to take a chance on me. Possibly, she was just desperate.

After I waved the family off to their holiday, I was surprised at how much free time I had. The three dogs needed walking twice a day and, as they were three very different sized dogs, this could take some time. The food routine was quite complicated and there was a yard to water, but it was not work.

I spent some of my free time exploring the local area and visiting family. The rest of the time, I wrote while the dogs sprawled at my feet.

I tried hard to be a good steward. I followed the routine the dogs were used to, and kept notes. These homeowners thought of the dogs as part of the family, so I wrote them a three-page letter about what the dogs had been up to during our time together, complete with photos.

I kept the house tidy, and gave it a good clean before the owner arrived back. Housesitting is a relaxed profession, but there are certain responsibilities and I take mine seriously. I cared for the pets and the house as if they were my own and I always made sure the pets were cared for before I went anywhere.

The homeowner was impressed and gave me a

marvellous reference that has been helpful ever since.

After completing my first assignment, I was more confident, so I accepted a longer assignment; six weeks at Tanah Merah, an outer suburb of Brisbane.

Two weeks before I was due to start, the woman called to cancel.

It was a bitter blow as it was to be my accommodation for the next six weeks. Luckily, I had family to stay with but I also learned to be more careful about which house sits I chose.

That one was organised by a daughter for her mother. I think the mother found someone she knew to look after her home and as we had not spoken, she did not have any problem cancelling me.

Most people are very reliable and this has never happened since, but I have become more diligent about confirming my position with the house owner and keeping in touch as time gets closer. After that experience, I also prefer to book house sits where people have committed vacation plans and have perhaps even bought their flight tickets.

***

My second confirmed house sit was in a suburb close to the first.

The owners were a young family who were travelling south for a vacation with family.

The owners did not want me to walk the two dogs, so there was not much more to do than feed them and keep their water bowls topped up.

I usually brought them into the house during the day while I worked. They would run in excited circles around the living room before they settled down to watch me while I wrote.

I washed, dried, and folded some clothes the family had not had time to do before they left and I kept the house tidy. Other than that, there was nothing to do.

***

The next house sit was not so simple. I had two small dogs in a house not suitable for pets. There were bars on the doors, rickety catches on all the windows and the toilet was across a landing cut off at night by a security door.

The dogs could not get down the stairs without me and used pads of paper for their toilet. Carrying smelly, sodden newspaper to the bin was not the highlight of my day.

The home was very close to the road, and one night I woke to the sounds of people leaving a nearby party. It was not terrible, just the noisy laughter and loud conversation of teens that do not yet comprehend that they are not the centre of the universe.

It took nearly an hour for the last car to speed out of the street and the last noisy reveller to stop talking.

I was tired and contemplating a sleep in, but the next morning I woke to what sounded like a neighbouring house alarm. About the third time I stood wondering when someone was going to turn it off, I finally realised it was one of the local birds.

***

I was keen to see as much of Brisbane as possible so the next house sit I accepted was out in the country. It was a six-acre farm, with two steer, a miniature pony, and an elderly dog. I anticipated a lovely quiet stay and some lovely windy country roads where I could ride my motorbike.

It was not quite like that.

First, my bike did not make the trip there and then my dreams of a quiet stay were shattered.

On the first morning, I woke to a low humming sound that I assumed to be a water pump. I was wrong.

I was staying in a remote countryside area an hour from the city and about five kilometres from the nearest shop. The road past the house only went to one other farmhouse, but someone was working on the road.

A man in a reflective yellow jacket was standing by my letterbox holding a road sign. He was as close as it was possible to get to the house without being on the property. I briefly contemplated the possibility that he was spying on me. It seemed so unlikely that he would choose the exact spot that was closest to my peaceful country hideaway

Then big trucks and yellow graders started to pass back and forth, vibrating the house with their low growling grumble. This went on all day until the workers went home for dinner. Then the day ended as it began, with an unusually loud jet passing overhead back and forth for a bit.

I called Phil for some sympathy. He said there was an air force base nearby; and it must be a jet out on test runs. So much for the peace and quiet of the country.

At that property, I had a few more jobs to do than usual. There was a garden to weed and water, a pony to look after, and land to take care of. The elderly dog just needed food, water and company and the two steer looked after themselves.

A week before the family returned, I decided it was time to mow the lawn. A note from the previous house sitter said that the mower was in the shed with the petrol. When I found the mower, it was the smallest rustiest looking mower I had ever seen. It even had four dollars written on it in white crayon.

I figured the father of the place was a fixer-upper like many men I knew, and put it off for a few more days.

The next evening I was on the phone when I was startled by a knock on the private back door near where the "obviously not a guard dog" lived. It was the owner's son.

When my heart started beating again, I asked him about the lawnmower. He showed me the shed where his family had a ride-on mower and a proper push mower. When the sitter notes said that the mower was in the shed they might have narrowed it down to a zone for me. There were ten sheds across the property.

The ride on mower looked intimidating and in any case, we could not get it started, so I decided the exercise would be good for me and started up the regular mower. It took me two days to finish mowing the football-field of grass around the property, but I had given my arms and legs a great work out.

On the second to last day, I decided to tidy up the four-legged lawn mower. I had never groomed a horse before and I was not sure what to do. There was an assortment of brushes on the bench, so I chose one that looked like a scrubbing brush and followed him around with it, while he wandered around ignoring me and eating grass.

Half an hour later, I had brushed most of his back and sides, and had even run the brush down his tail from a safe position away from his fidgety back legs. He did not seem to look any different but I was satisfied and proud. I turned to look at a passing car and he bit me on the arm. Ouch.

***

My next home had no pony and no grass. It was a modern two-story home and was long and narrow to make the most of the long narrow section. Around the house, there was only room for a path and garden border. There was a small courtyard at the back and a carport and small swimming pool at the front.

Entrance was definitely by invitation only. There was a key for the front gate and two for the front door. There were around ten glass doors that could be opened if it got hot, and each was also locked and bolted.

Inside it was a beautiful modern home set up as if Home and Garden magazine would be dropping by to take photos any minute. Each handsomely upholstered chair and carefully placed end table was strategically situated, and every knick-knack on every shelf was displayed with artistic flair.

My bedroom had its own living room as well as a bathroom. It was perfectly placed so that each morning, the sunrise would wash across my bed as it rose.

I didn't see many sunrises in New Zealand. Although we moved home many times, I was always on the eastern side of tall craggy hills.

Each morning in this home, I woke to a beautiful buttery yellow horizon turning to pink and salmon, and then to the clear blue that stayed all day. Queensland is magic first thing in the morning.

***

When I woke up in my next house sit, I was surprised to find freshly painted walls, and polished wooden floors. When I had visited earlier, I had the impression the house was old and tired. After I spent some time there, I realised why. The newness was only skin-deep.

The renovations had favoured looks over comfort

and practicality and there was a reason the woman of the house put the phone number for the plumber at the top of my list.

The toilet had to be flushed by pushing the lever a certain way or it would overflow and refuse to work at all. The showerhead sprayed water in every direction including straight up. I quickly learned to put my clean clothes out of reach.

Even a bath was not straightforward. I needed to boil a kettle of water to get it hot enough. The second time I took a bath, I had to boil three kettles of water.

The windows were the old wooden kind with loose catches. They looked like they might fall off if I opened them too far. The back door closed with a rickety door handle and a low sliding bolt, and the front door by a single key lock.

I spent my first night locked into my room, slightly nervous after coming from a house with screens on all the windows and a lock on the garden gate. The doors there looked like they could be jemmied with a credit card and two toothpicks.

To make it worse, there were no curtains in the living areas and I was painfully aware that someone standing in the right spot at night could see my every move.

After dark, I would creep around the house trying to avoid detection and I slept with my bedroom door closed and locked.

***

A few weeks later, when I moved into a rather run down inner city home, there was thunder. Fierce, loud, cracking, and break the sky in half thunder. It reverberated across the sky and lasted longer than any thunder I had ever known, even in Brisbane, the capital of spring thunderstorms.

I could hear the much more subdued rumble of planes taking off and landing at the nearby airport and I wondered if the thunder, and more importantly the lightning, would cause any problems for the planes. I had just been on holiday in New Zealand and was so glad I was not in a plane during the storm.

I had been very keen to get this house sit because the timing was good and the location very central, especially for the airport. I may have forgotten that it also meant I must get used to the overhead rumble of planes from a busy airport.

I was looking after the home for a tall serious looking young man in his thirties who had inherited the family home. He had two big dogs that needed care while he went to India to marry an Indian woman he met online. He was into meditation and Eastern Religion.

He had little white stickers on the doors, mirrors, and even the TV, that reminded him to chant, and long quotes from the Dalai Lama in the hall. His benches were lined with pictures of Indian Dignitaries and one of Jesus Christ. I made the mistake of asking if a particularly prominent photo was his fiancée. I think it was a young Indian goddess.

He had a pure water filter, beetroot powder, and Himalayan salt in his kitchen. There were boxes of no lactose milk lined up against the wall next to carrot juice, psyllium powder, and at least ten jars of dried beans.

As I arrived, one of the guests remarked on how tidy everything was. I know he had done his best to clean, but I had been spoiled. I found it hard to look past the crumbs on the coffee table, the spider webs on the windows, and the mix of boxes and congestion that lined the kitchen and hall floors.

The owner warned me his home was basic, and he was not wrong. It was very much, a young person's flatting situation. The gym he mentioned in his advertisement was a tired looking multi-gym unit in an alcove next to the TV. There were two substandard fridges, and a washing machine that needed a fork and a swift wallop to get started.

I liked my room, although it was basic and somewhat dusty. The sheets seemed clean and the bed was firm. It had unvarnished wooden floors, and an extra door to the living area which was blocked by the head of the bed.

There was another picture of an Indian Goddess on one window, and a line of bells on the other. There was also plenty of built in storage but most of it was still full of the belongings of the last tenant. I heard she went to India for two weeks and then just did not come back.

The owner hosted a Korean student, who rented one of the other bedrooms. He also had friend who slept over several nights a week, even when I was there,

It was very different from the peace, solitude and serenity of the previous housesits, but it was an adventure.

On my first night, the storm kept me awake and I could not relax. I wondered who had used the bed sheets before me and why the student insisted I should wear shoes in the house. I worried because there was no lock on my bedroom door and worse, no lock on the bathroom door.

A few weeks later, I was still having trouble sleeping.

It was not the student banging the heavy wooden door near my head as he headed out for his midnight rendezvous. It was not because he once left the door facing the street open a few inches all night. It was not because I had a broken window frame that could easily be lifted out, or even the gecko chirping gaily just through the paper-thin wall.

It was mosquitos.

I had always been attractive to mosquitos and one night they found me. I could hear one circling the room as its little buzzy motor wound up ready to attack as soon as I lay still. Without any bug spray, I had to take other measures.

I sat up in bed with my little headlight on until I heard it heading for my light, and then I whipped a small towel into a whirling, mozzie-killing, rotor. It seemed to be successful. As long as there were no hidden cameras in the room, poised to set me up as the next YouTube eccentric, I was happy.

The next night I was even sneakier. I knew I was a mozzie magnet, so I gave them time to find me in the lighted hall, left my light off until the last possible minute, and then jumped into my room, shutting the door before they could follow me.

Despite all that, something found me. I must have had my feet out of the covers for a bit, because by morning they were an itchy mess.

I also had bites on my nose.

I was plagued with red itchy spots, covered with raised red areas where I had scratched, and I had added another layer of unattractiveness to my poor blistered and dry feet.

I called Phil for sympathy. He just reminded me that the spots would go well with the three small motorbike burns I had also collected on my legs.

***

A week later, I tie-dyed a t-shirt.

It was all the rage when I was about ten. We tied strings around our t-shirts and then soaked them in dye. The string left pretty patterns on the fabric and the brighter the result the better.

This particular decoration had a charm of its own, but it was not intentional and it was not pretty, especially on top of the blue dye that had leaked from my jeans in the last wash.

Almost everything I owned was over a year old, including the jeans. Who could have anticipated they could leak any more dye at that time in their life?

I blamed the washing machine.

It was a front loader, and it tumbled the washing through a tiny amount of water. It was the one with the broken door and the pop out handle.

I had mastered the art of assembling the handle into the door and nudging it into place using a swift knee kick. The student had also taught me how to open it myself with the end of a spoon, but I obviously had the washing part wrong.

To add vivid insult to colourful injury, I had soaked a few items in with a tiny brown lace top the night before and it leaked onto my light washing in pink starbursts.

As I folded my washing, I was not impressed. My previously rose pink t-shirt was a blue t-shirt with pink patterns on it, and I had a matching pair of undies. Everything else that was any shade lighter than a circus tent was blue tinged with grey.

***

For the three weeks over Christmas, I house sat on the Gold Coast in a home conveniently situated between

Movie World and Sea World.

That house had something I had not seen since I was young. There was reading material in the toilet.

I quickly dismissed the fashion magazine with its images of impractical clothing on impossibly thin models, and chose the one with glossy photos of food and over four hundred barbecue recipes. This book was for real cooks and I found it intimidating. I am more of a food heater-upper and arranger.

I studied Heston Sausage with Mushroom Sauce. It had twenty-seven ingredients. Twenty-seven?

The first three ingredients were two types of meat and a surprisingly large quantity of meat fat. When everyone has been scraping the fat off his or her meat for years I wondered who even sold this? Perhaps it hides under the counter at the butchers, shown only to the select few who can quote Jamie Oliver on chickens and who know the names of all the MasterChef Judges. I also wondered if everyone but me had a grinder and a sausage-caser.

The house was definitely a girl's home. There were baskets in every room filled with make-up, creams, and hair products of every description. The woman of the house, although not much younger than me, was much more feminine. As well as lotions, and potions, and hair accessories in every room, there were forty pairs of high heeled and dainty shoes on a display stand just outside the door.

I was envious. I have never been able to feel comfortable in high shoes. As a child, I was a tomboy, and I still want to be ready to climb a tree or wade through a small stream at any time. Skirts and impractical shoes can make me feel nervous and trapped. I cannot relate to forty pairs of high-heeled shoes, but I loved the home.

I drooled over the art works. One of the daughters had drawn each member of the family onto a gold canvas. These five stunning pieces overlooked the formal dining table, while a large red and gold canvas that dominated the living room was painted by all five of members of the family together. The whole house fairly screamed family togetherness and harmony.

This was all the more impressive since it was a blended family. He was an Australian and she was from Indonesia. Their three daughters were a "hers, his and ours" grouping and they were all stunning. They reminded me of my own boys who range from the colour of dark chocolate to rice pudding.

***

It is a privilege to be inside someone's home. You know what food they keep in their pantry and what brands of toothpaste they use. You often know personal things, such as what they keep in their medicine cabinet or on their nightstand. You get a sense of their personality, not only by their taste in furnishings but also by the pictures on their wall and the books on their shelf.

You get a sense of what their community is like, by reading the community newspapers and advertising delivered to the letterbox. You shop where the locals shop and you often meet the neighbours.

Staying in other people's homes is a fascinating way to see how people live, but looking after their pets can be an adventure too.

Other People's Pets

Most people are cat or dog people, but I do not play favourites. I like them both for different reasons.

In my very first house sit, I looked after three very different and much pampered dogs.

The tallest was a German Shepherd, and the smallest a little terrier. This made taking them for walks interesting. I was constantly adjusting the leads to avoid tangling and we made slow progress. Each outing was more of a "search and explore" than a walk. They stopped often to sniff everything, and not all at the same time. When we did get going, I had to untangle the leads before we could start again.

Then there were the toilet stops.

We stopped for at least three toilet breaks and sometimes four. Each time I collected the result in one of the plastic bags I carried and hoped we were not too far from a bin. It was not my favourite part of the role and I varied the timing of our walks to see if I could avoid these stops by going earlier or later. I could not.

Those dogs had a very complicated feeding routine. There was dry food, canned food, and a piece of meat for breakfast, and cubed dog roll and biscuits for dinner. There were dog treats for when I went out, and meat bones for when they were in the garden. I don't think there was a single dog food that was not on their menu. The cupboard had even more options in an array of plastic bins.

That family treated their dogs as part of the family

and I totally supported their philosophy. Those dogs were the most relaxed I have ever met. They were gentle with each other and patient while I prepared their food. Not every house sit had such easy-going pets.

***

Some months later, I stayed in an old two story wooden home that was due to be demolished before the end of the year. My charges were two of the cutest white Maltese Terriers.

They looked like little fluffy toys, but they were fierce little fluffy toys. Their owner introduced her pets to me as stupid dogs. I did not agree. I think they knew exactly what they were doing.

I walked them twice a day in various directions, but we could not avoid trouble. We could walk past the small noisy dog that made my dogs yap excitedly, or the big noisy dog that made them yap, or the park where there were a variety of dogs that started them yapping.

When I first took them into the dog park, the other dogs, and their owners, all cleared out within two minutes. One owner explained that they were scared their dogs would eat mine. I could see why when one of my fluffy toys ran straight up to a Great Dane and yapped savagely at its kneecaps.

The house I stayed in was not their usual house. Their family home was undergoing renovations and they were renting for a few months.

The temporary home was not set up for pets. It had no fence in the yard and many steps. I needed to take the dogs outside regularly and carry the one I called the "Princess" back up the stairs.

I am not sure if this was strictly necessary but she thought it was.

The owner had warned me that Princess could be trouble, but they had been nothing but delightful, presumably because I was new. I was lulled into a false sense of security

One day, a few weeks after I arrived, Princess was outside on the balcony barking loudly, so I brought her in for the sake of the neighbours. She growled at me because she had to leave the little scrap of chicken wing bone that she had been gnawing on for almost two hours.

I took her into the office with me and placed her on one of the pillows the dogs used as seats during the day.

The other dog took one look at her and moved well away into a corner hidden under the hanging coats. She knew Princess better than I did.

Princess was looking unhappy so I leaned in to give her a little pat and she growled fiercely and bit me.

It was only my little finger, but there was blood. She carried on hissing and growling as I took her to the porch for some time out, grateful that she was small and fluffy, and not huge and heavy. That day, I changed my nickname for her from "The Princess" to "Demon dog."

There were two pillows and a folded quilt in each room, as well as little pet beds for them to sleep on in the bedroom. They still wanted to sleep on my bed.

One night, Princess padded around under the bed making her protest. Her little claws scratching staccato on the floorboards. I needed some sleep, so I helped them up onto the bed.

In the night, I woke to hear a slurping noise coming from Princess. At first, I thought she was licking her fur but when I gave up trying to sleep and turned on the light, she seemed to be slurping her tongue in and out of her mouth. It was a disturbing sound and not any easier to ignore when I could see what she was doing.

Because the light was on, the other dog decided to get up and head off to the living room. I was still having trouble sleeping so I wandered out to see what she was doing.

I was disturbed to find she had done number twos in the kitchen. It was 3am in the morning.

I went back to bed, but not to sleep. I was in bed with one dog that clearly did not know about toilet paper, and another still slurping like a blocked drain. It was a long night.

***

My next house sit was in an elegant home, all modern angles, tasteful art, and classic furniture, including twenty-three seats in the downstairs area alone. The two tasteful and elegant Burmese cats matched perfectly.

They were fastidiously clean and marvellously polite. They waited patiently at the door for me to let them in to, or out of, the house. One of them loved to walk along the high garden wall but she could not get back again. She would sit there quietly mewing until I happened by and lifted her down.

Like most cats, they tried to get between me and my computer when I was working, but what disrupted my concentration the most, was when they leapt onto the narrow balcony wall. It was two stories high, I would hold my breath while they did pirouettes and other fancy manoeuvres, just above what had to be a lethal drop, even for a cat.

One morning I served the cats their special canned food that looked like it would be quite at home on top of a bed of salad and served in a fancy restaurant. That day it was tuna and whitebait

I put on some classic French café music I found in the CD player, poured sparkling grape juice into a crystal glass and relaxed into one of the twenty-three elegant seats.

Then one of the elegant stylish cats sat on the elegant stylish stairs, licked her elegant paws, and puked up her breakfast all over the carpet.

I was sympathetic, as I have never been able to eat whitebait either.

***

The next two cats I look after were more alley cat than elegant. They lived like a pre-divorce couple. She lived in the kitchen and used the back door, and he lived in the front room and used the front door. Their food bowls were placed accordingly.

The owner insisted that they slept outside at night but the male cat liked my bed so I let him sleep there for company. Two days later, I noticed there was a dirty, greasy build up where he had been sleeping and sent him back outside.

Nearly a week later, he wandered in and got a particularly warm welcome from me. I had not seen him since he left and now I could stop speculating on how I would explain to the returning owners that I had lost one of their cats.

***

Dogs were just as interesting.

I looked after a gentle giant of a dog that lived in a concrete back yard and needed to go out for a walk twice a day. There was only one way to walk and, after two weeks, I was bored with it, so I covered the back of the borrowed station wagon I was using with thick tarpaulin and invited him into the car.

He had a marvellous time and was excited with the trip and the walk.

I had covered the car well but I had forgotten one important thing. He was a large slobbery boxer with droopy wet jowls and they were never wetter than when he was excited.

When we got back, he had exceeded all previous drooling records and I was not impressed. It took ages to clean off the back windows so I could see out of them again.

I wish I could report that we went for lots more exciting walks that involved car trips, but we did not.

***

My next house sit not only had two big dogs, but there was also a student staying there. I did not think that would be a problem as the owner said he looked after himself.

The two dogs ate from an old pot and, what looked like, a car hubcap. It turned out to be the battered lid of the pot. They drank from a bucket.

They lived in the laundry and were separated from the house by a rickety wooden fence that leaned against the wall drunkenly and was more of a psychological barrier than a fence.

The house was the noisy one, with planes that flew directly overhead and a speed bump right outside my window that made a passing vanload of bricks sound like the apocalypse. It also smelled like wet dog.

After a few weeks, one of the dogs became obsessed

with me. She tried to stick to me as if I was the only thing standing between her and death by loneliness.

She sat under my chair while I worked and followed me back and forth to the bathroom, the bedroom, the fridge, and the yard. I tripped over her many times but she was not deterred.

At 2am one night, I woke to the sound of her knocking down the childproof gate that was supposed to confine her to the laundry. I could hear her as she padded around the house looking for a way in to my room.

The second time she arrived at the door behind my head, breathing loudly like a scary phone call, I gave up trying to sleep and went to put her back in the laundry area. She stared at me with her saddest eyes, and flopped dejected to the ground. I felt so guilty.

Then the student started going out in the middle of the night. Since the front door was metres from my bed and the wall was thin, this was quite disruptive.

For a whole week, he had a phone call around midnight, then went outside, fired up his noisy little red scooter and zoomed off.

In the morning, I was never sure if he was home or not. I often lost count of how many times the door had opened and shut. One morning it was not shut at all. I woke to find the door wide open to the street.

I wondered if this had any relationship to the fact that he took three bottles of something alcoholic into his room some nights.

By the time I found my window screen had popped out and was laying on the ground outside my room, I was quite relaxed about the whole thing. If something were going to happen to me then it would probably have happened already.

***

Two Staffordshire bull terriers were my charges at the last house sit for the year. They had barrel chests, bandy legs, and were so bulky and clumsy I kept forgetting they were girls. They had appetites to match their bulky frames.

One had white socks and a white stripe on her chest but I could not tell them apart because the owners had insisted that I would remember that Nelly was the slimmer one. They both looked like sumo wrestler dogs to me.

From the minute I first fed them, they offered me their undying love. They desired nothing more than to slobber all over me and lick my feet. Luckily, they were outside dogs.

After I graced them with my presence and gave them some love while they welcomed me home like visiting royalty, I could leave them to fall asleep outside the door.

While I was writing, I often let them into the office where they slept as close to my feet as they could.

One day, I was too slow to let them in, so they made their own way in through a hole in the screen door. I was horrified. Was that there before or was it new? I left them outside after that and they showed their disgust by whining sadly.

In my second week there, I cleaned out the fridge.

This family had left the home as if they had just stepped out for the day unexpectedly. In the fridge was a large bowl of lychees in juice mixed with an unidentified jelly-like white fruit. There was a meat pasty, half a block of rum and raisin chocolate, and at least four open bottles of lemonade and coke. There were bread buns, rolls, and three kinds of cheese.

On another shelf, there was a large opened can of tuna, and a large amount of steamed rice still in its cooking pot in the fridge. I gave the rice to the dogs mixed with the tuna. Suddenly they came to life. They loved people food better than their dog food.

In the following days I offered them bread chunks, cooked potato and scraps of sausage and they discovered a completely new enthusiasm for their food

Who Needs a House Sitter?

House sitting is one of the best examples of a win/win situation that I have ever seen. The homeowner has someone to look after their home and pets while they are away and the house sitter gets free accommodation, power and a phone line.

Maybe you could be a house sitter. I have had some wonderful times house sitting and I can thoroughly recommend it. It is a fun thing to do and allows you so much freedom over what you do during the day that you only need to work very short hours to live like a king or queen. I love it.

Most of my families were away on vacation, but some were away on a working assignment, or visiting family. People go away for a variety of reasons. While they are away, they want the house to be as safe as possible.

Having a house sitter in their home allows them to relax, knowing that someone is there to look after everything, and to let them know if anything happens.

People put a lot of time, effort, and money into their homes. Even people who are renting might want someone in the house to look after their belongings.

Empty homes are a target for burglars and several people have shown me neighbours' homes that were ransacked while the owners were away. With a house sitter coming and going each day, the home looks occupied. There is probably a car in the driveway and shoes by the door. Someone is collecting the mail, putting out the rubbish, and turning lights on and off. When a home looks lived in, it is less attractive to burglars. Having someone in the home is peace of mind for the homeowner.

Some years ago, a friend of mine was on holiday and her husband thought he would be helpful and turn off the electricity while they were away. By the time she called me to go and check, there was a putrid, melted, maggoty mess in the freezer where hundreds of dollars of meat used to be.

A house sitter would have noticed the loss of power in time to save the food and avoid a nasty messy clean up.

Probably the most common reason a family will want you to house sit, is because they have pets that need walking or feeding. Kennel fees and pet motels can be expensive. A house sitter is a cheaper option for a homeowner with pets, and, since the pets do not have to leave their familiar surroundings, they are happier too.

I am mostly alone when I house sit and I like having pets for company. A dog will bark when I have visitors and motivate me to take a walk, and while some cats disappear for days, they are just as likely to curl up on my lap while I am watching TV or working on my computer.

Sometimes there are even unusual pets. I looked after two steer and a miniature pony on one small farm. I also met with a woman looking for someone to stay with about thirty goats, each with their own names and personalities.

They lived in the long grass in the fields around the house and were quite free to visit the neighbour's farm. I was nervous about that, especially since so many of them were due to give birth while the homeowner was away. I did not do that house sit.

If you would like to house sit and have farm experience, you should be able to find many opportunities for work. Farm owners are often looking for someone to stay over so they can get away for a holiday and might offer a small income for looking after stock. I have seen advertisements offering board on an organic orchard for a year and another asking for someone prepared to live in and help with a small bed and breakfast. One woman needed a house sitter for her vineyard so she could have some weekends away.

You never have to accept a house sit and can be as fussy as you like. Some house sitters only want to stay in a specific location or in a particular style of home. You can accept assignments for as long or as short as you wish. You could even accept an assignment that fits in with your vacation time.

People are good about leaving information about their pets and if they are comfortable leaving their animals in your care, and you have someone to call if you need help, there is no reason that you could not look after any kind of pet there is.

There are not many housesitting positions that do not include pets, but they do come up sometimes. I spent a month looking after a home just because the owners wanted the lawns cared for and the plants watered. In another home, they just wanted the house to look lived-in. If you do not like pets, you can still house sit, it just might take a little longer to find a suitable place.

I find other people's pets are one of the bonuses of house sitting. They make things interesting. When I am putting out the food for the cat, or walking the dog along a beautiful beach, I often think how lucky I am. Walk the dog, feed the cat, collect the mail, water the plants, and a little house cleaning. These are my jobs for the day and the rest of my time is my own. It is not a bad job, not bad at all.

For the house sitter, the benefits are many.

The first thing I love is probably all the free time I have. I used to be a manager for a large childcare organisation and I often worked more than the forty hours a week I was paid for.

Before that, I was a stay at home mother of six sons and ran the office for my husband (now my ex) while also holding down several voluntary positions.

As a house sitter, I have so much more time for my hobbies, my writing, and to help in the community.

Secondly, I love that the accommodation is free, as is my power supply and my landline. It saves me a lot of money. I only need a small amount of income to buy food and for transport.

Another of my favourite things about house sitting is that I get to live in a different area every time I move. There are new parks to explore, new shops to visit and a variety of local attractions.

I get to try out various suburbs before I choose one that might suit me as a permanent home. I have local knowledge of a number of places now. I know how long it takes to get in to see a doctor at Victoria Point and where to find the cheapest movie tickets in Brisbane. Most importantly, I know where to get the best hot chocolate on the Gold Coast *and* on the Sunshine Coast.

Staying in beautiful, interesting, or quirky homes can be another benefit of the job. I have lived high on a hill with majestic views of the southern Gold Coast, and another within walking distance of the Gold Coast theme parks. I have stayed in a brand new home in a new community and a run down and messy home with great character. I even stayed in a multi-million dollar home in a gated community with boat parking at the back door.

Each home was different, and all were educational.

I love seeing how people live. I think it is a privilege to be in people's homes and I learn so much from them. I get ideas that I will use in my own home when or maybe if, I settle down.

I see how cupboards are set up, which pans cook the fastest, and which kitchen gadgets are more useful than they look. I have tried the new induction stovetops and I loved them. I have used a variety of vacuum cleaners and washing machines. It is like my own personal consumers information testing system.

Often, I have been offered the use of personal items like a barbecue, billiards table, pushbike, swimming pool, or even a hot tub. People can be very kind.

One home had the most gorgeous artworks, and they were created by the family members. I would love that for my own home one day.

My house sits also introduced me to a variety of families and cultures, including Indonesian, Indian, Scottish, and of course Australians and New Zealanders. One day I would love to house sit in England or maybe France. It is such a good way to get right into the heart of a community and see how people really live.

I have also made some good friends among the homeowners. I might only meet them a few times but we can develop a bond based on shared interests and a shared love of their pets. Some have already asked me to return and house sit for their next holiday, another win/win for us both.

House sitting can provide many more opportunities than you might think and is an important service for people going away, particularly if they are going to be out of the country or state.

My families went to Scotland, Spain, Morocco, and Germany. A family with four children was heading for a six-week camping tour of the Australian outback, and a single man was travelling to India to marry a woman he met online.

All these people wanted someone in their home and a house sitter was a practical and an economical option for them and a cheap roof over my head for me.

So maybe now is a good time to talk about some of the practical aspects of house sitting. The next chapter explains where to find house sits, how to apply and what to expect.

Getting Started as a House Sitter

Being a house sitter is a good way to get to the heart of a community. You are not just a tourist, you are a resident. It is as if you are a visitor at the zoo, and instead of looking into the lion cage wondering what they do all day, you are right in there with them, sleeping in the shade, enjoying the hunt and sharing their meal, up to your elbows with juices running down your chin.

So how do you become a house sitter?

The first thing I suggest is an Internet search. If you type "house sitting" into a search engine, that will bring up a range of sites.

Look through a few to see what they have to offer. Pay particular attention to how many ads they have for the area you are interested in and check that they are getting new ones in each month.

Try to work out how many are current. Many times homeowners forget to remove their ads when they have already found someone. You might see a large number of ads but if they are past their start date, they are probably filled.

There are sites that charge house sitters and those that charge homeowners. I prefer a site where I have to pay. If the homeowners get free ads, you should have more to choose from.

Some sites charge you a different rate based on which ads you want to view but I find an annual fee that lets you access all homeowner ads in a wide region is better. I have become a gypsy and even though I prefer Brisbane now, I do not want to miss any good options in Cairns or the Whitsundays.

Most sites will also have an area to post your profile. Many more people approach a sitter from their profile than put out a public ad, so set one up early. Look at other ads for ideas on what to say.

Try to tell homeowners what you can offer them and what will make you different. Do you love animals, are you fanatically clean, or are you home during the day for security and as company for the pets? Have you been a professional cleaner? Have you taken care of any friends homes?

Look for things that make you stand out as reliable, tidy, and honest. Emphasise your skills. When I housesit with Phil, his maintenance experience is a real bonus.

Approach it like a CV, and make it look and sound professional but friendly. Have someone proofread it so there are no spelling or grammar mistakes.

Obviously, experience helps, but it is not essential. Advertise confidently but honestly. If you do not love pets, do not pretend you do, just emphasise what you can offer. Try to work out what advertisers are looking for and meet their needs.

After your first housesit, ask for a reference. Having one will help you stand out if there are several applicants for the house sit. Get as many references as you can, and also ask homeowners if they are happy for you to give their number to families that are considering your services. Once you have references, mention this on your profile.

Many families are concerned about the security of having someone in their home. A reference helps reassure them that you are not going to run off with their big screen TV.

A criminal records check is another useful item to have. In my more than a dozen housesits, only one family asked for a criminal records check, but if I had not had one, they would have chosen someone else.

If you find a house sit you want to apply for on a website, you will probably need to pay your joining fee if you have not yet done so. This will give you access to the homeowners details. Plan your application email to the homeowner as carefully as you do your profile.

Keep it brief and friendly. Tell them what you can offer and why you will be best for their needs. If they have a dog, tell them about your own dogs or experience with dogs. If they want garden care, tell them about your green fingers. (If you do love gardening of course)

Don't be too discouraged about people who do not reply. Sometimes people get scores of applications. It is fine to follow up if you do not hear back but be friendly. They may have been away, offline or they might have filled the role or changed their plans. I have probably had no response to about half of my applications. Be patient and apply again.

When you get a response, you can ask them the details of their property and pets, and offer to visit if possible. Homeowners are reassured when they can meet you face to face, and you can meet the pets and see what the house is like. If the home is far away, you might offer to phone or talk to them on Skype.

Take along, or email, any references you have and maybe even copies of your police check and your driver's licence. Most people do not need them but are very happy to have them.

Find out what day, and the exact time you need to start the house sit, and find out when they plan to return. If they can give you copies of their itinerary, it might be helpful.

One homeowner contacted me while he was away to tell me he had given me the wrong date and he would be home a day later than expected. I was due to leave for another house that same day, so I said I would stay late and feed the dog before I left.

It turned out that he had the date right the first time. He arrived home to find me still in my pyjamas, with everything I owned piled up around the door. He was apologetic, but I might have been better prepared if I had been given a copy of the itinerary.

If the family offers you the house sit, and you are happy to accept, they may ask you to fill in a written contract. Only one of my homeowners wanted a contract but it can be a good idea and you may like to suggest it yourself.

Your home sitting website will probably provide a good template or, if you are not already a member, you could go to the Aussie House Sitters website and get one by joining their site.

Before the family leaves, find out as much as you can about your responsibilities. Most people will leave notes when they go. You need to know what the animals will eat, and at what time of day; where they sleep, and whether they are allowed to sit on the furniture. This varies between homes and pets are like children. They will try to get away with as much as they can.

Ask for emergency numbers or contact emails in case of problems. Who will you call if there is a flood or other emergency? Do they have a vet they prefer you to call if the pets get sick? Do they want you to email them with updates during their trip?

Ask about their phone plan so you know which calls you can make for free and which will attract charges. You should make arrangements to pay for any calls outside their free plan.

If the house sit is for three months or longer, the homeowner may ask for a contribution to these costs, or request that they be paid by you. Make sure you know who is paying for these costs upfront.

Before you move in, most people will show you how to operate the TV, the oven, or the washing machine. I find I can usually work these out for myself but I always make sure I find out which day the bins need to go out to the street. I do not want them to come back to several weeks' worth of smelly trash.

I provide all my own food, toiletries etc. but I ask if they are happy for me to use their spices and sauces. I do not carry these things with me and it helps provide variety in my meals. I also check what other items they are happy for me to use. Often they suggest I use any vegetables or herbs that are growing in the garden.

I also do not use items like hot tubs or barbecues unless they have been offered.

When I move into a house, I sometimes take photos. They are a good reminder if I forget how things were set up when I arrived and might also be handy if there was any dispute.

I try to minimise my impact on the home. I take note of where things like pots and plates come from so they can go back in the same place. I keep everything as close to how it was left as possible, then just before I leave, all I have to do is to do a last minute clean of floors and surfaces etc.

The owner should return to a home that is clean, tidy, and welcoming. It should look the same as it did when they left.

I also like to wash the sheets and towels I use and, if I know what they like, I buy milk or bead for their return.

I prepare notes with details of anything they need to know like phone messages that came while they were away, or maintenance issues that cropped up. In one house, I had to let them know they had possums in their roof, and in another, it was a snake in the ceiling.

Sometimes I stay for the owners return and other times I leave the home before they get back so they can relax. I ask them what they would prefer and am open to change. Either way, I make sure they have my contact details in case they need to ask me anything later.

If you choose housesitting as a lifestyle as I have, you may need to consider what you will do between housesits. If you have your own home, or are in a long-term housesit, this will not be a problem for you, but otherwise you need a backup. It is not always possible to find a house sit that starts when the last one ends.

I have slept in my station wagon on a few odd nights, but mostly I stay with family for a short time, or take a trip back to New Zealand. One time, I had a ten day break, so I went on holiday to Cairns. It still worked out cheaper than paying rent and was much more fun.

When people ask me how I got into house sitting. I tell them I signed up for a housesitting web site, paid my fee, and sent off applications. It really was that simple. Since then I have had fourteen housesits and lots of adventures for that original fee. That is a good deal.

House sitting can be a cheap place to stay on a holiday, or a way of life as it has been for me for over a year. It costs very little, but you do need some money, so let us talk money next.

Supporting Yourself

I have a confession to make. I may not be the best person to tell you how to support yourself in style. I have plenty of ideas and some of them are great ideas but I would not have had so many wonderful experiences without Phil's generosity. My bike and my phone were gifts from him and he paid for my trips to Nelsons Bay and back to New Zealand.

With that in mind, I am happy to tell you how I managed to feed and clothe myself. Then I will offer some other ideas about making money and living on a limited budget.

Before I left for Australia, I applied for an Assistant Manager role at a health retreat that would allow me to live onsite. A week before I left, I still had not heard back but I was strangely confident that it would be okay. I told my friends I was probably going to end up renting a broom cupboard in Brisbane. Phil told me there were many great bridges in Brisbane. I could live under one of them.

I put everything from my little flat onto Trade-Me and prayed for the best. Just days before I left I had raised eight thousand dollars by selling everything in my little flat. I sold everything from ten dollar books and scrapbook magazines, to the two thousand dollar couches that were less than a year old.

It never occurred to me that I would return. It just felt right to leave everything and go.

Two days before I left, the retreat finally called to confirm that I could stay with them. This was to be my accommodation and my income but it turned out rather differently than I expected.

The centre was as unorganised as their late response to my application would seem to suggest. On my first morning, I was not sure what to do or even who could help me. The person who had accepted my application was away for the week and had left no instructions.

No one seemed to know why I was there so I started by helping in the kitchen. I was not impressed by the dingy placemats and stained cups and glasses, or with the young man who was washing dishes in dirty water.

Late morning, the retreat manager decided to send me to the office at a nearby location. No one there knew what to do with me either, so after more delays and more confusion, I became Bob's assistant.

Bob was large, loud, and enthusiastic. He told me I was his best and prettiest assistant yet, but he told everyone that. My first job was to spend all morning making appointments with potential clients so that Bob could "chat" with them. Frank did not seem to keep any of the appointments.

He would charm, coax, and sometimes bully people into signing up for a stay costing thousands of dollars a week. He promised sad, addicted, and lonely people, an eighty per cent success rate. Some of the facilities he offered were not available, and I suspect he made up his own statistics.

I stayed in a room attached to the retreat living areas and ate the same food as the paying guests. It was a lovely lifestyle and I loved meeting the clients, but the lack of structure was difficult. I started each day helping with morning outings and tidying up after breakfast.

After that, I would just turn up for work and try to work out what needed doing.

On the second week, the manager asked me to sit with a recovering alcoholic in the evenings. She was a lovely woman and we got on well, so the next week the manager asked me to move in with her.

I was surprised to learn that I was her support person in the evenings. My instructions were just to be there and not to talk to her. For this, she was paying thousands of dollars a month.

I was very sad when six weeks later she packed up her things and left the retreat. I heard she went straight to the pub on her way home and started drinking again.

On my third week, one of the managers asked me to start making sales calls. I declined. I was already working at the retreat all day, and staying up with the alcoholic client at night. I had not had an interview for the assistant manager role and I did not have a job description. Worse still, I had not received any payment.

The manager looked at me as if I was crazy. I think she expected me to be available at any hour of the day just for the privilege of being there, but I was quickly running out of goodwill for a centre that had not lived up to its promises.

Finally, I was offered an allowance of $100 a week and board. It was not much but I decided to stay for the experience. Toward the end, I even worked as a kitchen hand to get petrol money for my motorbike.

When I left the retreat, I did not apply for a real job for two reasons. First, Phil had arranged for me to go on a motorbike rally with him, and secondly, I wanted to be able to travel to see Phil and to visit my sons.

I started to look for something I could do as I moved around.

Phil was supportive as I considered my options and discarded them one by one. I wanted to provide something important and useful to the world, but I could not decide what that should be. I was not very productive for a long time.

I spent many hours working on the details for a possible party supply website. I had some success selling online children's party supplies some years ago but things had changed. There were so many great online stores doing that now that I was not so sure I had anything to offer.

I applied for a few jobs from a mail carrier to a high-level manager, but found it hard to muster any enthusiasm for working for someone else after my previous experience in the work force.

I considered life coaching. I had coached a few people as part of my training and they seemed happy with the results, but I was not sure I believed in the system I had been taught.

I decided to sell yacht supplies online because Phil had just bought a yacht. I thought it was something I could do while we cruised around the Mediterranean or across to the Pacific Islands.

I designed a website and gathered a long list of wholesale suppliers before I realised I did not know much about yachting and I lost confidence and interest.

I set up a web site about Australia and I made just over eight dollars in just a few days. It seemed like a promising start until a month later when I still only had just over eight dollars.

I read everything I could find about making money online but nothing seemed to stand out.

I found out that the best way to make money online was to sell programs about making money online. You buy the program so you can sell it to someone else, who sells it on.

They were mostly useless or out-dated reports that people were buying so none of this would work for me. I wanted to deliver something useful to the world.

I learned a lot about the people making money online when previously expensive online systems started being given away free as part of a way to promote new online "opportunities". I tried a simple system that cost me nothing and earned me nothing.

I collected everything I could get that was free and learned enough about the Internet to write a short book on the subject and to be glad I never spent any money on any of these systems or reports.

After two months working all day on the computer, I still had no income and was out of ideas. I still did not have a job and I needed somewhere to stay.

Then I remembered an article I read years earlier about people who did not pay for accommodation. It was an article about house sitting.

After several months of staying with family and getting nowhere financially, I sold some shares so I could continue to feed myself and I moved into my first house sit.

That took care of my accommodation and the first few weeks but I needed an income. Phil suggested I concentrate on my writing, so I started writing about my adventures. It was fun, but it was not going to be profitable any time soon. I looked at other options.

Finally, one of my nieces told me about a job she was doing from home and helped set me up with a small income.

I called business owners and set up appointments for a salesperson to go and talk to them about free training for their staff.

People were mostly friendly and some were quite

chatty but as I had been a small business owner, I knew I was interrupting their busy day.

I only worked a few hours each day and I made enough money to buy food each week. It was perfect for me while it lasted. I appreciated the job and the income but it didn't last long.

About six months after I started housesitting, I moved into a remote rural property. I went to set up my computer and found that the modem was missing. All the connections were there but the actual modem unit had gone.

I called the owner. She knew I needed the Internet to work from home but she had forgotten. She had exchanged the home modem for a mobile one to use on her trip. This was a big problem.

As well as my work connection, the Internet was my phone book, atlas, cookbook and TV guide. It was my connection with friends and family.

I was so grateful for Phil. When I was still whining an hour later, he started teasing me about all the sites I would not be able to visit and the information I wouldn't be able to look up on Google until I realised I was being unreasonable.

While Phil and all my ex colleagues were slaving away at their desks, I would be cash poor, but I would be on a three week holiday on a small farm in a beautiful part of sunny Queensland. Suddenly it did not seem so bad.

This house sit was a particular struggle, but it was also a good experience. I got plenty of fresh air and exercise and I learned to relax without the Internet. I also learned to live on less than most people would consider pocket money.

When I was back online, I tried a bit of mystery shopping. I would buy takeaways or talk to someone about phones and then put in an internet report about the service and the facility. Between four and six weeks later, they would reimburse me and pay a few extra dollars for expenses.

It took me almost an hour to fill in those first reports and I had to spend time doing online training too. It paid very little for the time it took.

I was never going to make enough to survive, but it did get me pocket money and a few free meals.

I tried online surveys, but the ones I did, pay around three dollars for a fifteen-minute survey. It got me a few supermarket vouchers in six months but since there were only a few suitable surveys a week, I was not going to survive on that either.

Eventually I settled on article writing. I got fifteen to twenty dollars an article and it would have been even more successful if I had worked at it more often. Instead, I went exploring, visiting, and having adventures. At least that gave me plenty to write about.

The biggest boost to my budget came when I applied to deliver census forms. It was a short but lucrative job, and it gave me enough to survive on quite nicely for about three months.

It has not been easy to get casual work to support myself but that has been because I move around to suit my family and myself. If you want to support yourself on the road, here are a few options that might work for you.

If you plan your times, you could follow the harvest trail and help with everything from cotton picking to pruning grape vines. The Australian Government has a job search website that includes a range of casual harvesting and farm jobs. (See the references in the back of the book)

If you are a performer, there is always the option of

busking, although you might need permission in some places.

You could sell items as you move around. Some people sell items they make such as fresh homemade bread, home sewing, or hand-made soap, and market them via the internet or to local stalls. Other people carry a supply of items that they buy wholesale and sell retail.

If you have a skill that is in short supply, you might find work for a few weeks. You could also apply ahead to be a short-term dishwasher or cleaner.

Approach an employment agency that specialises in short term roles and see what they can suggest. If you find a house sit for a long enough term you could even get, or keep, a regular job.

I have chosen to live on an extremely low budget because I love the freedom. I have raised six children and had a busy life until now so this is like a sabbatical for me.

I do not mind going without sometimes, but an ongoing income is only half the problem. I can enjoy it more because I have alternatives and a backup plan.

On days when I am agonising over whether I can afford a new notebook or a three-dollar pair of socks, it helps to know I have emergency funds and a long-term plan.

If you are considering an adventure like mine, here are some suggestions that will bring you peace of mind as you travel.

You should have something to come back to when you are ready to settle down again. I have a small investment property where the rent covers the outgoings and I still own almost half of the family home. Once my ex-husband buys it from me I will buy another investment property and start building up more assets for my retirement.

You also need short-term plans. If you get sick and need medical care or the car breaks down while travelling, you need access to immediate cash. I have a few more shares I could sell, and I have supportive friends and family that would help in an emergency. I also have basic medical cover and a roadside rescue plan.

It would be better to have money in an emergency fund, but as long as you know what your options are, you can relax and have fun knowing you have back-up if anything goes wrong.

I am a risk adverse person, so having something in place for an emergency helps me enjoy the challenge of living on a strict budget. Without a back-up plan, living cheap is just poverty, and that is no fun.

I became very tight with my money and, because it was temporary, I enjoyed the challenge of eating well for less.

One day, through the magic of markdowns, I bought two lunches, two breakfasts, chocolate, and bread all for six dollars fifty. I became a master bargain shopper and was enormously pleased at what I could get for a little money. It is surprising how much satisfaction I got from a few weeks living this way

Coles mark down everything from yoghurt, to juice to pasta and they use nice big stickers. I once got a pasta lunch for a dollar, two yoghurts for just over a dollar and pesto dip for fifty cents. Regular specials can be good too. A can of baked beans was sometimes only a dollar and made two good breakfasts with some low cost bread.

I learned to visit the supermarkets late in the day. There were often discounts and markdowns on cooked food and sometimes meat. I one got a chicken sandwich dinner for just one dollar and it was big enough that I had some left over for the next day.

Most of these items needed to be used the day they were bought so I only ever bought what I needed. I also did not buy anything that was not in good condition. Good health is important even when eating cheaply.

I often took a bottle of water and snacks with me so I did not need to pay expensive prices when I was hungry. Movie theatres, shopping plazas and airport food stores are all bad places to buy food. When my budget was particularly low, I avoided cafes or bakeries too and made my own sandwiches and occasionally, baked goods. If I was hungry when I was out exploring, I might buy fruit, nuts, or fresh bread from a supermarket.

I think allowing yourself some treats is important. Mine was usually dark chocolate or corn chips. They gave me the feeling I had indulged myself, and yet there are good things in dark chocolate and corn chips are not too bad for me.

I tried to have five servings of fruit and vegetables, and a small amount of good quality protein like chicken or fish each day. I often found small cuts of meat for just a few dollars on special in the supermarket and made it into a soup with whatever vegetables I had. As well as being good for me, one pot often lasted several days. You probably already know that soup is often better the next day when the flavours have had more time to blend.

In most of the places I have stayed, the families have offered me anything that ripened in the garden and the use of pantry items like salt, pepper, herbs, spices etc. This extended my food options and meant I had less to carry with me as I moved. I replaced anything that ran out before they returned.

One week was particularly dismal. I was house-bound because I was recovering from the flu and my motorbike was waiting for repairs.

I needed to get to the shops but they were a thirty-minute walk away and I could not face it. I was still feeling tired from the flu and I had a headache.

It was the second week of solid rain and my clean clothes supply was down to a t-shirt and a few pairs of socks. I did a load of washing and sent a prayer of gratitude that this house had a drier.

My food supplies had become quite critical. I was down to one egg, a small bag of carrots and a good amount of grated cheese. I had already raided the family's supplies, which amounted to a packet of cheese crackers and some ginger nut biscuits that I would replace before I left. There was not much else there I could use.

I eyed up a can of pea and ham soup but it looked a little old. After finding out that the baking powder expired in October 1989, I was reluctant to take the risk. Even if I could face eating it, I might not have been able to find a replacement can of the right vintage.

I proved to myself that it was possible to find anything I needed on the Internet, by finding a suitable recipe for using carrots with cheese.

By using chilli sauce instead of chilli powder and adding balsamic vinegar, just because it seemed like a good idea, I came up with a very tasty soup that I liked so much I made it twice.

After five days of rain, there were signs of sunshine but I still could not go out. I had a headache all weekend and it continued for days. I thought it might be my pillow, or the way I hunched over my computer all day, or my increasingly bizarre diet.

After almost a week of being confined to the house, I finally felt well enough to venture outside again.

The mystery shopping company had tracked me down in my new location and asked if I would do a few assignments. They even offered a few extra dollars. I had nothing better to do so I accepted.

I spent my birthday morning at a central city plaza talking to Telstra about new cell phone options.

The bus trip cost five dollars and took an hour for the return trip. The online reporting took another hour. I got eleven dollars back after seven weeks so I made around six dollars for two hours that day.

The next morning I did a mystery shop at a fast food place. There was a small thrill in knowing that they would be more attentive if only they knew who I was.

The young person taking my order seemed confused and the place was messy. When I returned home, it took me more than an hour to write my report so it sounded unbiased and fair.

When I was done, that was another five dollars earned for about an hour and a half of my time. If you add in the cost of bus fare, there was no money in it at all. It was just a free breakfast and another day out.

I enjoyed living on a limited budget, but I am an adventurer at heart and at my happiest exploring. I was home most days writing but sometimes I wanted, or even needed, to get out and do things.

Living simply meant doing without many things, but never fun. I have had more interesting adventures than I could ever have imagined a few years ago.

Adventures for Free

I stood in a Brisbane City square, looking for an Indian festival but there was not a single colourful sari in sight, just busy city people crossing the square on their way to important meetings.

I took some photos of the statues and wondered if it had been postponed because of that morning's thunder and lightning storm.

I met up with one of my sons for lunch and he commiserated with me about the missing festival. Then I called my other son to ask what he was doing for his birthday the next day.

It was then that I found out I was a day ahead of myself. It was Thursday, not Friday.

It was not the first time it had happened but it was the first time I had done it so publicly. I could see my sons laughing and swapping stories about their mums failing faculties.

The truth is that I do not often need to know the date or even the time. While most people plan their lives around jobs during the day and TV schedules at night, mine is much less predictable.

Some days my "To Do list" reads; eat, write, and exercise.

If there are pets in the home, they are my first priority, but after that, I am free to go out as often as I like.

The next day, I travelled back into the city for the

festival.

A community event like this is a great night out for the cost of a train fare.

There were musical acts and Bollywood dancers. I even got dinner for three dollars when I bought a fried onion pancake from one of the stalls.

It was entertaining and interesting, and it was exciting being part of the crowd. You just cannot get this experience by watching it on TV.

Brisbane, like most cities, has free outdoor movies, exhibitions, and displays most weekends. I never went into town without seeing some interesting event such as juggling street performers, vibrant pavement artworks, or groups of young people tag dancing in a circle.

The weather in Brisbane is perfect for evening activities, but even in windy Wellington where the winter winds come straight from the Antarctic, and rain falls horizontally, there is a small window of summer and outdoor events.

In Wellington, I went to a free rock concert and sat among the rowdy excited teens. I went to a free symphony orchestra performance and made friends with the people nearby who were elegantly dressed and obviously cultured and well informed.

I went to a presentation about the Easter Island theories, and a display of Da Vinci models, and an art festival where I watched painters working on canvases amongst a jostling crowd and watched pictures made of dazzling light beams projected onto the art gallery wall.

I attended free outdoor Tai Chi classes at a Gold Coast park, and free digital scrapbooking classes in a Redlands library. I have had free dance lessons, free cooking lessons, and been on free guided bush walks.

For a small fee, I could have gone to belly dancing classes or pottery workshops, or sailing classes.

Getting out and having fun is just a matter of finding out what is on in your region or it might be just being in the right place at the right time.

One afternoon on a damp Brisbane day, I headed to a large park to watch two teams compete to place a goats head on a stick while the opposing team tried to stop them by hitting out with blow up weapons.

I read about this sport, called Jugger, when I was discovering a new park. They said it had an international following. Australia has a national team but this was the first I had heard of it.

They seemed to be ordinary people who had a not so ordinary way of spending a Sunday afternoon. The goats head was made out of fabric and the fearsome looking weapons were not dangerous, just annoying.

One giant of a man, with a giant blow up club was having an exciting time as he ran around whacking everyone on the opposing team, but most of the others were more relaxed.

Another man was sitting on the ground throwing small stones at a large metal gong. When he reached a hundred the game was over.

It was all fascinating and just another example of how much there still is to learn, even at fifty years old.

While big cities have almost constant activities, small towns have their own charm. I love the relaxed pace of a sleepy little town where the claim to fame is a statue, a lake, or even a vegetable. Perhaps the queen of England once visited or Ned Kelly rode through. I love getting to know more about these small regions.

It is like getting to know a person better and appreciating their personality and character.

Then there are the unique festivals.

I ate lamb and potato pie at the Lamb and Potato Festival in the small town of Guyra, and hot dogs at the country fair in Mudgee.

I was disappointed to miss the Melon Festival at Chinchilla and I was nowhere near the pig diving festival in Melbourne but I would love to go one day. I definitely have to go to the camel races or the Beanie Festival in Alice Springs.

I get most of my information about what is on from the Internet. I have signed up for emails promoting the latest local events but I also get ideas from the local visitor information centres, city councils, notice boards or even newspapers. Spend some time researching what is on and you will find a wealth of free activities.

Even on a small budget, I am never at a loss for things to do, often for just the cost of a train fare.

If there is a charge for an event or attraction, I might ask if I can take a quick look inside to see if I will want to come back when I can afford it. Most of the time, they say yes.

I visited the highlights of the Sunshine Coast that way. I bought an ice cream at the Bli Bli Castle, had a hot drink at the Bellingham Maze, bought bottled water near the Aquarium and some ginger scones at the ginger factory. The only one I actually visited was the Ginger Factory. I travelled by motorbike so even the transport cost very little.

There are so many wonderful things to do for free that I rarely felt the need to attend a paid event. I love parks, museums, river walks, bridge crossings, and botanical gardens. I explore city parks, majestic old churches, mind stretching museums and sometimes back alleys, just to see what is there.

I love being out exploring, especially on a weekday. It has the feeling of playing hooky from school. Sometimes I just wander around looking at things that interest me.

On the days I did pay for an attraction, I was not disappointed.

One day I visited the railway museum. I spent five minutes in front of the ticket office reading all the advertising brochures and still could not decide whether I should spend almost twenty dollars for a ticket. I knew I could buy a few days food with that money, and I badly needed new socks and undies.

I also felt guilty enjoying it alone when my sons might have enjoyed it.

In the end, my life philosophy won out.

I imagine myself as an old person confined to my bed. I want to have many delicious memories to savour. When I can't explore any more, I want to know that I made the most of every opportunity I had.

I bought the ticket.

I found it surprisingly enjoyable. There were only a few other people there and I was on the group tour alone, but the presenter did not miss anything out. He explained the difference between a tank engine and a tender engine (this stayed in my head for about five minutes) and then the difference between an A, B or C class engine, which has to do with the number of wheels.

I sat in the cab of a diesel train and a tilt train, and played train driver as if I was ten. I examined electric coils, and learned how the new trains glide using magnets and opposing forces to keep them balanced. I climbed on and off the full sized trains, and spent the day as if I was a child enjoying a day without adult supervision.

I went to the café for lunch and was surprised to see the sandwiches in the cabinet only came in large catering packs. I asked for something smaller and the woman at the counter said she could make me any kind of sandwich I liked. I asked for a crocodile sandwich and she said she was sorry but she did not have any beetroot. I found it immensely funny.

I consider that money spent on experiences like this was a good investment, but most of my adventures were free as long as I could get there.

I visited China Town in the heart of Brisbane City. It was a kaleidoscope of the sights, smells, and even sounds of Asia. There was not much English being spoken there. I felt like I was having the experience of foreign travel for the cost of a train fare.

There were so many unusual foods. I would have liked to select my lunch from one of the curry stalls or maybe try a kebab. I was almost salivating over the Japanese cone shaped pancakes filled with everything, from tuna to strawberries with cream, nuts, and caramel sauce.

I would have liked to try some of the shiny red barbecued duck displayed nearby. It hung glistening in the windows of several shops alongside less attractive parts like roasted duck livers, and a huge plate of ugly duck claws. I took photos of dead ducks and assorted parts. It seemed somewhat creepy.

Instead of trying something new, I ate a fast food hamburger because, it was a mystery shop assignment and I would get my money back.

Even getting to an event could be an experience. One day a small group of teenagers boarded my train wearing blood covered clothes and painted on scars. They wore wigs, hats, and several items designed to look as if they were buried in their head; knives, pins, even a computer keyboard.

A few were holding awful looking blood spattered dolls that they held by one foot or squashed to their chests. That must have given the children on the train nightmares.

As the sky darkened, I saw hundreds of bats flying silently past the train. It all looked so surreal and it was not even Halloween until a week later.

I assumed it was just another young person's party but later I saw it on the news. Thousands of people took part in a "Zombie Walk" through town and the event raised over ten thousand dollars for the brain foundation of Australia. Now that was fun with a purpose.

When you are in an unfamiliar house, it can also be fun to stay at home.

I stayed in a home that looked out over the southern Gold Coast beaches and rivers. The view was so beautiful that it was an attraction in itself. Another home was in a gated suburb that had its own security, street services, and road cleaners. It was a big community and it took up to ten minutes just to get as far as the gate to the outside world.

The gated community had other advantages. One night Phil tried to turn on the light and pressed the emergency button instead. Two minutes later a security team turned up and insisted on searching the house from top to bottom. Perhaps they thought he had someone tied up in the broom cupboard.

A security response like that can be very reassuring.

I also enjoyed my time with the pets I cared for. They were fun to walk, play with, and to cuddle. I wrote most days, so I was often home for the pets and we became very attached, especially if we were together for longer than a few weeks. I met some beautiful and interesting animals.

Each new house brings new experiences and a few challenges. Each time I move, I have to learn my way around again.

In New Zealand, I had a nice old brick of a pc cell phone that I had inherited from a previous job and it stopped working just before I left for Australia. Phil replaced it with a marvellous phone that did, and still does, everything except dial itself. It has the Internet and a GPS voice we call Marvin.

Once I installed the right software, Marvin helped me find my way around by say things like "At the next intersection turn left" or "In three hundred meters at the roundabout, take the second exit."

Marvin was heaps of fun and good company. On my travels, I saw some rather creative ways to get places.

One day he bypassed the motorway and took me up the steep and windy incline of a local hill. I ended up taking the longer scenic route and arriving with an almost empty tank of gas and a big smile on my face.

Another time, he knew I had passed my turnoff, so he calculated a new route. I assumed he would send me back. He tried to send me another twenty-five kilometres around the mountain. Luckily I noticed in time.

Other times, the GPS allowed me to follow byways and back roads and trails with the assurance that when I had finished playing, Marvin's instructions would help me find my way home.

The first time I used my phone map was when Phil and I first flew into Brisbane and we were looking for the retreat. I was excited to power up my new phone GPS and we headed north out of town as per my instructions.

I was looking at a tiny map on my tiny screen and hadn't yet set up the navigation tool. I had to keep scrolling across the map to see where we should be going and saying things like, "We turn left at the next intersection, or maybe the one after that," and, "Wait, I am not sure. Hang on. Maybe it's the third intersection." Luckily, Phil is exceptionally patient.

***

One day I took a long hot walk thanks to Marvin.

I was walking down a long, wide, road between industrial buildings and enormous office spaces. I was hot, tired, and confused. I thought I knew where I was going but I did not.

I was on Ann St and looking for the Central Station that was on Ann St. I could not see it, and there was no one to ask for help except a woman in spandex shorts and a t-shirt.

We had been standing at the last set of crossing lights together and she had taken off like a demented duck. Her arms flapped out to the side, and her head rocked wildly as she ran.

It is possible she had a motor coordination disability but I suspected she had other problems. In any case, I would have had to run to catch her and I was too tired.

Marvin, my GPS should have been more helpful but he was still "thinking." Sometimes he takes his time locking in to our position, and that day was one of those days, so I kept walking, hoping to spot something familiar.

Luckily, I remembered my hat that day. If there is a sophisticated sun hat for city wear, I have not seen one. I was wearing a baseball cap and I past worrying how I looked.

I angled it to try to shade my face, but it was barely helpful. In the network of concrete paths, and concrete roads, between giant concrete buildings, that was that part of the city, the heat of the sun was beaming from all directions.

I did ask a woman back in the city if I was going in the right direction but she answered a phone I didn't hear ring and ignored me completely. I spent at least ten minutes ruminating on her rudeness and might just have been a little distracted as I set off using my own initiative to decide a direction.

I was wrong. I ended up in unfamiliar territory, wondering where the central station had gone. Marvin finally kicked in. Apparently Central Station had gone to the other side of town.

Luckily, I was not too far from another station so I tried not to look too tired and decrepit as I trudged up the hill past the people sipping cappuccinos in the shaded café and made it just in time to catch a train that not only headed back to the city, but also went to my current home station.

I suspect I will find myself in that part of town again and I will say to Phil, oh yes, I know where we are; I came here once on a walk. Phil will just smile and shake his head. He won't even ask why I would walk in such a dull out of the way place. He knows me too well.

***

One day, Google Earth and Marvin sent me to a road that ended abruptly at a small but un-crossable dirty brown river. The road started again on the other side.

The next day, a local gardener was kind enough to point out the location of a bridge on the other side of a wild and overgrown grass field. The field was ringed with barbed wire and I wanted to know why.

He insisted it was for horses. I visualised myself

running from bulls while shouting "but he said it was safe."

The field turned a corner and there was a bridge. A padlocked gate blocked my way.

I had come this far, so I climbed through the rails, onto the bridge, and walked across to the other end.

As I crossed, I counted four mud-encrusted shopping trolleys half submerged in the dirty water. I stopped to take photos and wonder why this happens so often. Who roams around a remote grassy field with a shopping trolley and then decides it needs a swim?

At the other end there was another locked gate. I climbed over.

There were horses to the right, so I took a sort of trail to the left and found myself wading through sloppy mud where the horses had churned up the wet ground. I was glad I wore flip-flops, especially when one foot sank so deep into the mud that I nearly lost it.

I had to stand on boggy ground to lean across boggy ground to pull my shoe back onto damp ground.

At the other end of the track, I was relieved to see a road and an industrial area. I stared blankly at my GPS to see where I was. Across the road, a man in a utility vehicle was looking over at me. I knew he wanted directions. That was so ironic under the circumstances.

I was in dirty jeans with my hair blown into a rats nest and mud all over my shoes and feet.

The camera hanging from a strap around my neck was probably all that stopped me looking like a homeless person. If I had only washed off one of those shopping trolleys, I could easily have been mistaken for a bag lady.

There was a huge noisy delivery truck waiting to get out of a nearby driveway so I could not hear the man and he could not hear me.

I waved my GPS at him in an effort to convey that I was unable to help but he finally managed to say that he just wanted to know the direction of the city. He thought it was left and I did too, so I sent him off in that direction and heaved a sigh of relief when Marvin, my "GPS when he feels like it," decided to come out and play and I found that I was right.

Half an hour later, I reached the river and another new park. I was so glad to have Marvin, even if he often makes me wait.

It would not be as much fun if I had to carry a map around. The most popular book of Brisbane maps is the size of a big city phone book.

I also use Marvin for my favourite game called geocaching.

Geocaching is a sport that uses multi-million dollar GPS satellites to find little plastic containers in odd places, and Marvin cheats.

The Global Treasure Hunt

One morning, I followed Marvin's directions and he led me to a garden inside the grounds of a small old church. I was hunting for some kind of small container and I could not see it. I looked for quite a while until I became suspicious of the water sprinkler. It was the only one there.

I opened it up and found it was a fake. Inside was a little roll of paper with lots of names on it. I was so happy to find it. It was my first since I learned about the sport of geocaching a few years ago.

I wrote my name on the paper to prove I found it and when I got home, I logged into the geocaching website to share my find. This was just the beginning of many adventures for me.

If ever a pastime was made for a house sitter, Geocaching is it.

Geocaching is a sport where people hide a container, called a cache, and then publish the coordinates so others can find it using their GPS. There are over a million hidden all over the world and over four hundred in Brisbane City alone.

I love geocaching. I get excited when my satellite signal leads me to a little plastic pill container in a tree, or an ammunitions can, in remote bush. It is a fun sport and once you have your GPS set up, it is free. You cannot get better value than that.

I have found lookouts, and bush tracks and

waterfalls. It is a great excuse for exploring new places and is a great way to get to know a new area. After searching for a few weeks, I usually know my way around the area better than many families who have lived there for years.

It works for me because there are new geocaches to look for every time I move. Looking for them usually leads me to the most interesting attractions in a community.

Marvin has fun too.

Often he leads me to within ten metres of a find and says, "That is all I am going to do. Find it for yourself."

Sometimes, like a petulant child, he refuses to come out and play. Other times he leads me into a wild and remote forest. Then he shuts down completely, leaving me to hunt in a wide area of overgrown tangled bush.

I curse and fume sometimes, but I enjoy the challenge.

In Mudgee, I found a huge, curved, and striated rock called "The Drip" and an aboriginal artwork called "Hands on Rock." The rocks at each site were stunning. Some rock faces were deeply pockmarked like giant blocks of Swiss cheese and another formation was tall and pointy like a collection of castle turrets.

I would not have found them without geocaching.

Most of the time, I also found the little container with the logbook to sign.

One day I was hunting for a geocache in an overgrown gully when it began to rain. I had checked beneath every tree trunk and rotting log in a wide area but I still had not found the cache.

By the time I gave up and headed out to buy a consolation hot chocolate, I had damp stringy hair, muddy shoes, cobwebs on my clothes, and almost certainly the odd spider or two on my person. I was surprised they let me in the store.

There was hardly a trace left of the sedate and sensible manager left, but there was a huge smile on my face.

Then one day, I attracted unwelcome attention.

I was lurking around an empty playground while Marvin took me back and forth in one direction and then another. One of the neighbours seemed to be watching so I had the phone to my ear, hoping she would assume I had stopped to make a call.

I narrowed the goal zone down to an area between some bushes and the fence. It was obvious by the trampled groundcover that others had done the same thing.

The cache took a while to find because it was partly buried, so it was some minutes later before I emerged from the undergrowth and headed back to my car.

The neighbour was sitting on a chair on her front lawn.

I assumed she had seen people here before and was suspicious. She was definitely making sure I knew she was watching me. I tried to smile and wave but she seemed unimpressed, as she took out her mobile phone, presumably to report something.

I was sure she recorded the number plate of the car I had borrowed from my ex and wondered if the police would contact him about this.

I quickly headed off to another cache in the same suburb. I had just seen it when a young boy came over and offered to show it to me.

He said his neighbours all knew about the cache because they already had the police around to take it apart and look for drugs. I signed the log and made another quick getaway.

The next day I saw a group of police in my street as I went out for a walk and hoped it was not connected. After being reported to the police in Dunedin as missing, I did not want to get into any more trouble.

Spiders, Birds, and Half a Snake

Like many New Zealanders, I thought I would see kangaroos at every turn, a koala in every gum tree and I would have to dodge snakes, crocodiles, and dangerous spiders every time I left the town.

I never did see a koala in the wild, but I saw many kangaroos. They were usually grazing on a golf course. They must have been a nuisance, but I think they like the short grass.

There was never much chance of seeing crocodiles either, as they don't live in the areas where I stayed, but I did see a snake; at least, most of one.

I spent hours poking around in the undergrowth, around trees, under bushes, and sometimes inside hollow logs, looking for geocaches. I was often nervous, and a little hopeful, that I might disturb a snake.

When I finally did see the little brown snake, it was just the tail end. It was slithering away through the long grass as quickly as it could. It was a small thrill but I got out of there very quickly.

That brought my "Australian wildlife seen in the wild" collection to a few hundred kangaroos, thousands of beautiful birds, ten water dragons and various other lizards, no koalas and half a snake. It was no consolation that I had seen plenty of spiders.

One night in Maleny, I found a large black hairy

spider in the living room. As the only other occupant of the house was a recovering alcoholic paying around thirty thousand dollars a month for her stay, I felt obliged to deal with it. I went after it with a broom, intending to sweep it into a dustpan and let it free outside.

It took off running along the wall like a demented and fluffy crab.

I did the only thing I could think of. I grabbed a long handled broom and kept poking at it until it was maimed enough to slow down and then brushed it outside. The next day I found it dead under the deck chair.

Another night we had what I can only describe as a spider explosion.

On arriving home, I found thousands of tiny spiderlings spread all over the guest bedroom ceiling, walls, and even on their bed. Every inch of wall on all sides of the room was covered in the tiny intruders.

We moved the affected couple and their bed into the living room and I cleaned up as best I could, smearing the spiders along the wall with a wet cloth. Housekeeping brought in their mops and buckets the next day, but the couple did not stay a second night.

Spiders are not the only furry things I have seen,

One night, I was walking home in the dark.

There were no footpaths and the trees hung over the road. They looked pretty in the daytime and like something from a horror movie at night. Something bulky rustled the trees as I went by and made me jump. It was probably crows, but I wished I had the dogs with me.

I was walking in the middle of the road to avoid the tree things and suddenly, I saw a long dark shape up on the power lines. It looked like a rat. I could see its long tail and make out the light shining off its fur.

I grabbed my phone camera to try to get evidence. The rat thing took its time and meandered along as if I was not there. By the time I had taken the camera off video mode, taken a flash photo of the air half way up to the power lines, turned off the flash and then decided video would be best after all, the rat had disappeared out of sight and I had no evidence.

I was disturbed by the fact that the power lines must be a sort of highway in the sky for wandering rat like things; and they led into every home in the neighbourhood, including mine.

I hoped that, should a rat invade my place, the little dogs I was looking after would treat it the way they treated big dogs and annoy it to death with their yapping.

The quantity and variety of wildlife in the city surprises me but the countryside has its own charms. One day, I stayed on a small farm and took a walk along a country road.

The trees were twisty and wild looking and it had been raining so there was water in the streams and in puddles next to the road. Along with the many birdcalls, there was the insistent drone of buzzing insects that sounded like intermittent and muffled chain saws.

There were termite mounds and duck ponds, little muddy creeks and fields of tall dry grasses. There was a farmer on a tractor ploughing his field while about twenty crows circled noisily and landed on the freshly turned soil as he passed.

I stopped to explore a cemetery and found an unusual tree that seemed to be hung with pictures of pears. They seemed far too flat and shiny to be real, but on closer inspection, they turned out to be pairs of green seedpods.

I found a group of what looked like sausage trees. They had huge dark green canopies festooned with hundreds of long dangly strings with bulbous sausage like pods dangling off the ends.

Then I found a green bike helmet strapped to a tree with a plastic egg inside. It was also home to several earwigs and a colony of big black ants that bite. I know this because I stuck my hand into it to get the geocache hidden inside. I still had an ant climbing around under my jeans ten minutes later.

There were tree-studded paddocks with cows of muddy brown or patchy black. They turned to watch me pass, still chewing lazily on tufts of grass. Then there were the two steer on the property where I was staying.

I was happy to see them as they were part of my stewardship at the farm, but they were less than happy to see me walking along the dusty road toward them.

They watched suspiciously, then turned quickly and ran off when I got too close. Then they attempted to hide behind a few lanky trees.

They had to weigh four hundred kilograms each and I was amused that they were scared of me. They seemed to think I would not see them behind a couple of scraggy old trees.

When I finally arrived home, there was an enormous rabbit on the front lawn. It looked like a kind of deformed wallaby with the hindquarters of a small kangaroo and long furry ears.

I expect the locals would be unimpressed but I rushed straight for my camera. All I got was a photo of those enormous back legs retreating and two blurry shots through the window. I went outside to set up a better angle but it was gone. Like the yeti, it will remain a mystery to me. I wonder if it was a hare.

I find Australian scenery and wildlife endlessly

fascinating and, despite the biting ants and the fist-sized spiders, it has not been as dangerous as I assumed before I came here.

I wake up some mornings in the soft blackness of the pre-dawn and listen to the magic sounds of the birds. I try to count the species of birds I can hear and often there are just too many.

There are squeaky toy sounds backed up by the little staccato tweets and chirps and twitters of smaller birds. Sometimes, there are at least six different choruses.

In the blurry state between dreaming and consciousness, I once thought I was listening to someone whistling a country music song with squeaky back-up music.

I have often stopped to admire groups of birds, emerald green, crimson, scarlet, and gold, often all on the same bird. Startling splashes of pure white might mean cockatoos. They fly in large boisterously cheerful flocks, feasting on tree flowers and leaving a trail of empty seedpods.

I found out why the Australians use the word "galah" to describe someone who is cheeky and irreverent when I watched a flock of galahs hamming it up on the power lines. They were pink and grey with little antennae tufts on their heads that made them look permanently startled.

In New Zealand, I only ever saw these birds in cages. I hate seeing birds in cages.

In some homes, I had regular visits from a surprising variety of birdlife that homeowners had encouraged to visit by offering food.

In one home there was a huge collection of birds that arrived each morning to be fed. There were cockatoos strutting and barking as if they owned the place. They would eat the black sunflower seeds that I put in a bird feeder in the garden. Scores of pigeons sat on the roof and then flew down and covered the road when I threw out budgie seeds. Two kookaburras and a magpie with a banded leg visited the balcony each afternoon and I fed them tiny portions of specially prepared minced meat.

You could go a long way and pay a lot of money to have an experience like that at a zoo or Wildlife Park, or you could take care of a home and have birds come to you. It is just another bonus of the job.

The Little Yellow Motorbike

When I first met Phil, he was about to embark on a motorbike rally. Afterwards, he sent me photos of his bike in front of mountains and out-of-the-way cafes. I began to dream of adventures like that, but I did not think it would happen.

I was not an adventure seeker. I was the mother of six and a grandmother. I stayed home and read books, or went for sedate walks.

A year later, Phil was preparing for the next motorbike rally in Tasmania and he was keen for me to join him. I was not in a position to buy a bike but I trusted Phil to work it out and he did.

One day I when I was working at the retreat, he sent me a text. It said, "I have bought you a motorbike."

His confidence in me was stunning. It had been almost thirty years since I rode a motorbike and I had been a regular at-home mother since then. I did not have adventures; I planned them for my boys.

The last time I rode a motorbike was almost thirty years before when I was living in Samoa. I had seen many accidents since then and age and experience had made me more cautious.

Phil was also cautious. He bought me a jacket, helmet, boots, and reinforced gloves. I looked like a real biker and was ready to roll.

The yellow motorbike was the start of something

wild and wonderful. It made me feel adventurous and interesting before I even rode it. It was also an incredibly practical and generous gift.

When I received it, I was staying in Maleny, a rural community with almost no public transport. The bike gave me freedom and the ability to explore greater distances, but first I needed a learners licence.

The woman in the transport office was not helpful. She said I could not get a motorbike licence without a Queensland licence. To get that, I needed an invoice with my name on it to prove I lived in Australia.

She insisted that any bill would do, telephone, electricity or rent receipts. I had trouble making her understand that I had none of these, even though I lived in the area. It was the first time I realised that having no fixed address could be a disadvantage.

After three frustrating visits, she told me that I could get a statutory declaration from my employer. Luckily, I was still at the health retreat. If I had been housesitting, my "employer" would be a family away on holiday.

I had one motorbike-riding lesson in the car park of the Big Pineapple, a Queensland attraction that has few visitors on a weekday. Later Phil followed me around by car for a weekend. After that, it was up to me to get more confident alone.

Maleny was a beautiful area to ride a bike, with its gentle hills, and lush green dairy farm pastures. I went riding as often as my schedule permitted.

I discovered just how heavy my bike was when I dropped it trying to do a slow turn on slippery gravel. After I stared at it uselessly for a few minutes, I figured it would not lift itself up so I would have to attempt to break my own previous, admittedly puny, weight lifting record.

I removed my helmet and tried to remember which way I was supposed to turn the wheel when lifting the bike. There was a short struggle and lots of grunting. By the time I finally got it upright, I felt like celebrating. Then I found out that it would not start.

I did not know what else to do so I phoned Phil. He assured me that it would just take a minute to settle after being on its side and naturally, he was right.

It was useful information when I dropped my bike a second time while trying to make a turn on a wet grassy paddock in the middle of nowhere. There is no dignity in lifting a bike while your boots slide muddy grooves into the grass.

The cost of the bike lessons and the licence was over four hundred dollars but thanks to all my practice, I was somewhat confident of a pass.

I followed my bike trainer down the windy mountain roads of the Glasshouse Mountains and up through the flame tree lined streets of Buderim to his office in a bike shop. We passed a girl riding in just a t-shirt and shorts and he signalled to me his disgust.

He sent other hand signals and I totally misread them. I was supposed to ride toward one side of the lane and I spent the whole trip riding confidently down the middle, even when he wagged his fingers at me. I just waved back.

He also signalled me not to run over the metal manhole covers but I could not fathom his meaning so I nodded, assuming he was pointing out something interesting.

I spent twenty minutes watching a safety video while he replaced the clutch lever on my bike, presumably broken when I dropped it earlier. After answering a short easy questionnaire, I had my pass.

I took full advantage of my new license. I headed

north one day and visited the ginger factory about an hour away. I drove home down the coastal road and got happily lost. I visited the aquarium, a castle, and the Etamogah Pub, a cultural icon. I visited and admired but I did not go into any of them because I was short of money.

I found out that I do not mind riding in the rain when it is so warm, even though the rain hits with the force of a pellet gun due to the speed of the bike.

I discovered that when the sun came out the warm air rushing past would dry my jeans quite quickly except for the area around the crotch. I got a few odd looks when I got off my bike.

I also found out that the police will not give you a bike registration when the mechanic has put just one wrong number on the safety certificate. It meant another long trip into Maroochydore in the rain.

I loved riding, so even the damp day could not curb my enthusiasm. I was happily heading into town on a six-lane motorway when a flashing siren came up behind me.

I was only doing seventy-two kilometres an hour but the limit was sixty. I found that hard to believe but have no choice but to accept a traffic fine.

I had not received any money from the retreat by then and the bike licences and ticket had been expensive. For the next few weeks, I worked all day and then washed dishes in the evenings to get some pocket money, but I was having the time of my life.

I was exceedingly cash poor, but I had Phil. He was, and still is, the world's most wonderful boyfriend and he had signed us up for my first big motorbike adventure.

The Motorbike Rally

It was a warm and damp evening in Devonport as we lined up with a hundred other bikes and riders to get off the ferry from the mainland.

First one bike roared into life and then another until all the bikes were revving up together in a tumultuous chorus that echoed around the belly of the ferry.

There were several hundred bikes there, and because many of them were taking part in the same Ducati motorbike rally, most of them were red or yellow. It looked like a packet of M & M's has been scattered throughout the cargo hold and someone has eaten most of the blue and brown ones.

We left the ship in small groups and lined up on the dock in huge long queues waiting to be processed.

A man on a tall blue trail bike pulled up next to me and we began a conversation. He said he was also there for the rally and I was reassured to see I would not be the only one not riding a Ducati.

He said he had been caught in the Victorian bush fires and that he had a bad arm. I was not sure that I heard him right and looked at him blankly. He lifted his left arm with his right hand and dropped it uselessly back against his bike jacket.

He showed me that all his bike controls were on the right side of his handlebars and I thought about how hard it would be to control everything including steering with one hand. I had to admire him and it made me feel more confident. If he could manage the rally with one hand, then I could certainly do it with two.

I was slightly uncomfortable as we drove our bikes in and out of the town traffic following Phil's friend. It was a quick pace and I was torn between being happy she assumed I could keep up and slightly terrified of sliding into an undignified heap at the side of the road.

As we negotiated the unfamiliar streets, I was oddly relieved when she stalled at a red light. I thought it might make it less embarrassing when I had my own bike mishaps.

It grew darker and I was tired and disoriented as we headed out onto the highway at just above the speed limit. My night vision is very poor but I had to keep up or risk becoming separated. There was also my pride involved.

I could not see anything past the end of my headlights and knew I could be just meters from disaster but it was also exhilarating. At one point, I could smell the sea nearby but it was only inky blackness outside the beams from my headlights.

It was a relief to pull into the town of Penguin where we were staying the first night.

The next day Phil and I headed out along the coast road to Stanley. A large monolith of a mountain towered over the town so we took a ride on the chairlift to the top and enjoyed the sweeping views. We bought fish and chips from a shop with a huge crayfish on the roof and a hundred more swimming in tanks inside, and then shared the chips with a one legged seagull on the grass by the water's edge.

We rode out to a forest park near closing time and Phil tried to persuade me to go on the giant tube slide.

It was long and curved, and disappeared at a steep angle down into dismal swamp.

The operators promised it was so fast that the 110-metre ride was all over in seconds.

We compromised.

Phil agreed to try it so I could enjoy it vicariously. I am not as adventurous as I sometimes like to think.

I ran down the meandering forest path just in time to get a blurry photo of him emerging from the end of the tube at one hundred kilometres an hour, with a big smile on his face.

We had a quick look around the forest floor and then because the park was about to close, we accepted a ride back up the path in the cart that transported the ride equipment.

It was an adventure in itself. The guide shared witty anecdotes while we bounced up the narrow rock-strewn path perilously close to rock walls.

***

The next day, we stood at the side of the road eating ripe cherries while the juice ran down our arms. We admired the murals at Sheffield and visited several funky museums. For two dollars each, we marvelled at shells that ranged from the tiny and delicate, to the huge and spiky; all in a myriad of glossy colours, including the occasional neon lined pastel.

There were seaweeds, and urchins, and enough sea treasures and boat bits to keep us laughing and pointing for almost an hour. For such a small room it was good value. I love it when something completely unexpected surprises and delights, especially when it costs so little.

We crossed the road to an odd little drapery shop

that was set up to look like as it might have looked fifty years ago. There was a life-sized model of the original shopkeeper sitting in a booth high on the rear wall where he would have been able to see everything.

Dockets and money used to be ferried to him on a flying fox type arrangement that was still there.

We headed out of town to an attraction called Tasmazia. It was not one maze, but a series of mazes with things to discover around every corner. We wandered around hand in hand and pointed out all the oddities to each other.

We got lost in the reproduction of the maze at Hampton Court and ran along the low wall maze. My favourite was the nursery rhyme maze. There were witty quotes and silly puns at every turn and a whole village of little houses dedicated to contemporary and historical issues.

***

Exploring together was fun but we were there for a rally. On the third morning, we headed down to the Launceston Park where it was all excitement as several hundred bikers milled around half listening to welcome speeches from the local mayor.

I noticed several categories of bikers in the rally. There were the super casual who were just there to have a good time and the super organised that had come hoping to impress. They often had shiny new looking bikes and slim, pert, almost haughty looking women that seem poured into their leathers, perched on the back. Some of these women looked uncomfortable and awkward, as if they had come as accessories, or decoration for the bike.

I made the mistake of asking two such couples at a

petrol station whether they knew the way to the meeting point. It seemed they had trouble deciding if they did or didn't, and how much they should convey to this ordinary looking woman on a little yellow bike that was not even a Ducati.

Despite those who were there to impress, everyone seemed friendly and there was a lot of cheerful banter as we waited for the rally to begin.

Phil and I could not hear the welcome speech so Phil dragged me closer to the sound until we realised we were heading for the loud speakers and he had positioned us almost on top of the mayor.

People were starting to wonder if we were part of the show. Thankfully, the speeches ended before we were too obvious and everyone headed for their bikes.

The sound of hundreds of motorbikes revving up was thrilling and I could not believe I was part of it. We waited patiently as we watched hundreds of growling bikes head out of the park, parting to avoid the one bike that did not start first time, and head off into the town.

When the speed demons and boy and girl racers had left, we joined the more casual group near the rear.

We rolled noisily through a town full of people brought to a standstill by our passing. Traffic officers waved us through red lights and past motorists stranded on side roads.

It was a parade of sorts and I had this bizarre urge to wave at all the people standing wide eyed on the sidelines.

I resisted since I was really the least likely to be of interest. As well as not being on a flash and shiny Ducati, I was probably riding the only bike there that could be ridden by a ten year old.

Out of town, we hit what turned out to be one of the best parts of the ride, a narrow tree covered road that wound up through a forest to a lookout.

Among all those bikers, I felt powerful and alive in a moment of pure pleasure. With the wind in my face, riding sometimes felt like flying.

Some impatient riders zipped past at dangerous speeds but for the most part, I kept up with the main groups and found myself being held back by a few who were even less confident on the corners than I was. It was exhilarating.

After the first stop at a lookout, the group split up and, as Phil would say, we "diddly-bopped along" doing our own thing.

As we rolled into each town, we saw groups of bikes parked outside the cafés or more often the pub. The riders were often sitting drinking on verandas and porches and we speculated whether some of them might have been doing more drinking than riding.

Phil rode his powerful new 1000cc bike sedately behind mine for almost the whole rally. I urged him to take off and have a run that was more worthy of his bike and thirty years of experience, but it was not until the third day that I saw what he could do.

A young man on a bike came roaring past us and suddenly Phil was gone. Within seconds, he had disappeared up the narrow windy road and I caught glimpses of the two sets of red taillights as they dodged in and out of sight at break-neck speed.

It was thrilling watching him effortlessly weave up the narrow windy road. When I eventually reached the top, many minutes later, he was waiting for me and smiling. He is a humble man and I had to ask several times before he admitted that he won the race.

***

On the third day, the police set up roadblocks but there would be no ticket for me on this trip. I had trouble coaxing my little bike to go past eighty kilometres on the hills and I reached my top speed of one hundred and twenty only on downhill runs. Even then, the wind had to be behind me.

We rode through fields of high grass that had attracted what must have been billions of tiny white butterflies. My jacket and helmet had already built up a thin layer of squished insects, but in that section, for every few feet I travelled, there were hundreds more tiny massacres. I tried not to think about it.

Not long after that, I felt a stinging sensation in the neck of my jacket. I suspected it was a bee so I flattened my jacket against my skin and hoped that I had squashed it.

I had not. I felt more stings.

I caught up with Phil who was now ahead of me and asked him to stop. He smiled and nodded, and carried on riding.

After several more minutes and several more stings it was clear he had forgotten. I stopped at the next available spot and ripped off as much of my upper clothing as was decent.

Phil finally noticed I was missing and returned. He had not heard what I said and was apologetic.

I had seven raised red blotchy stings on my neck and spent the rest of the week trying not to scratch and not really succeeding.

My favourite part of the ride itself was a wide sweeping section of curved road. I enjoyed being an active participant in the ride, leaning the bike to one side and then gently rolling out into the next wide corner.

My least favourite part was the last straight steep

hill where I urged my bike onwards as it got slower and slower and reached the top all hot and sweaty and gasping for breath. The overheating light came on and we had to stop and wait for it to cool down.

***

Tasmania is a stunning and varied showpiece of an island. We rode up to four hundred kilometres a day through a variety of landscapes; from craggy mountains, to ancient forests, to gentle farmlands. We stopped at small country towns and at anything else that looked interesting.

We discovered a footpath lined with bricks inscribed with the names and a few details of convicts who arrived here many years ago.

In Campbelltown, I tried a thick grey seafood soup with a strange name I forgot right after I had given my order. It looked like a lumpy wallpaper paste but it tasted delicious.

We stopped for honey ice cream, and hot chocolate, and always cold drinks, lots of cold drinks. The weather was hot, and while riding was comfortable, every traffic light and stop on the road was warm and sticky.

Each evening we had a communal meal with the other hundreds of people on the rally. One night we gathered at the Axe Mans Hall of Fame to eat and then watched some woodchoppers in action.

Another night we stopped at St Helens and ate overlooking the ocean. The food was buffet style, spread out across several tables, and by the time Phil and I arrived, several tables had already been picked clean.

There was mumbling from people who had been to past rallies and thought this was not as good, but I was having the time of my life.

***

On the last touring day, we crossed the stunning Tasman Bridge into the equally stunning city of Hobart.

Phil lived in Hobart for six months while he was training for his time in Antarctica, so we visited the Antarctic training facility where I admired the stunning life-sized photos of life in the Deep South.

We strolled through places like Salamanca Point and Battery Place and admired the beautiful stone buildings. They were built by convicts who had been shipped from England for offences ranging from stealing a loaf of bread to murder.

We rode our bikes up to a lookout over Hobart. The road was narrow, windy, and steep. It was also wet after a day of rain that we missed.

After four days of riding around Tasmania feeling like a professional rider, I lost power on a corner while trying to adjust for a car coming the other way. My bike dropped out from under me.

The bike was laying head down in the slippery leaf litter at the side of the road. It was too heavy for me to lift in that position so I was left sitting helpless and embarrassed, waiting for Phil to come and help me.

Phil was helpful and reassuring. "It can happen to anyone," he said. He knew it was not a good time to tease me.

We had dinner at the Drunken Admiral where the walls were lined with old bottles, spyglasses, pirate skeletons, and other memorabilia of the sea. We ate fish and chips on a boat tied to the wharf, and on the last day, we joined the rally group for a red and black themed dinner where we all dressed as pirates. My friends would not have known me.

I have given speeches to audiences of over three

hundred people and trained large groups in media and other subjects, but I have resisted dressing up my whole life. Ask me to wear a silly hat or take part in a role-play and I am suddenly shy and awkward.

After riding over a thousand kilometres on my motorbike, I was a new woman. We ended our trip to Tasmania by wearing big buckles, pirate hats, and menacing stick-on tattoos on our arms. Even better, we had a vibrant, happy, rollicking old time.

***

On our last day in Tasmania, we had to ride back to the ferry, but there was just enough time to visit one of the wildlife parks.

As well as kangaroos and koalas, I met wombats and Tasmanian Devils. There were birds too. I was embarrassed to find out that the beautiful photo of kookaburras I was so proud of, was actually a family of tawny frogmouths. Phil was amused.

We had a marvellous week, but there was not enough time for all the attractions I wanted to see. I did not mind missing the golf museum, the gold museum, or the mining museum, but I was so sorry to miss the chocolate museum. It closed just minutes before we arrived.

I was also devastated to miss the umbrella museum. It sounded so quirky and I reminded Phil often of my disappointment. He thought I was joking, but I was not.

The week felt like a triumph. I had only been riding my bike a few months and I had already completed my first motorbike rally. I was officially a bikie.

I did not see that coming, but I am glad it did. It was just the start of many marvellous travels on my little yellow bike.

On the Road

The fields along the Australian roadside are usually a dry brown with sandy coloured grass, but on this trip there were some bright green patches. New shoots were growing in the curved furrows of the newly ploughed fields. The bright, almost lime green of these fields, contrasted nicely with the dry dusty red brown of most of the scenery.

I was riding my motorbike from Mudgee in New South Wales to Redbank Plains in Queensland to see my new grandson. It was to be a two day, eight-hundred kilometre trip and my first motorbike trip alone.

I had not done much riding since getting back from Tasmania two weeks before and I had Phil with me then. Fortunately, the excitement of being on the road was enough to overcome any nervousness.

Phil had fixed my bike and put on new gauges and I was feeling tentatively confident.

I went through Coolah, which proudly advertised itself as the home of the black stump, although it did not seem to have a stump. On the way out of town, a flock of galahs swooped down around me and just for a moment, I was almost riding inside the flock.

I followed a trail of model planets part of the way but only saw Jupiter and Saturn. I think the other planets may have been too small to catch my eye.

I made it all the way to Goondiwindi before dark and arrived just in time to visit the information centre for some help in finding a place to stay.

When I asked the man at the desk what I should do in town, he apologised for not being available to take me out on the town. He said he was already seeing a woman friend that night.

Perhaps he thought I was suggesting a date but I was not sure why. It was an information centre designed to dispense traveller information. I could have been flattered but he looked older than my father.

The towns claim to fame is a horse that once came second in the Melbourne cup, so the guide insisted on showing me around the horse themed museum. I took a few photos and tried to feign an interest.

Later, I booked into the cheapest hotel in town. It was the usual two story wooden building with wrap around verandas and lattice cornices. By the utility trucks parked outside, I guessed it was a favourite with contractors.

It didn't seem like it tried very hard to attract tourists.

My room was compact, shabby, and not too clean. There were cobwebs on the ceiling and pieces of crumpled up rubbish behind the little brown fridge. The sheets were clean, but thin enough to see through. There was an air conditioner but it sounded like a biscuit tin full of rocks.

I spent the night alternately freezing and cooking, depending on whether the air conditioner was on or off. In the morning, I threw open the balcony doors to get some of that beautiful Queensland sun that I had missed and there was a contractor smoking on the shared balcony. It was not one of my better nights.

I could never have imagined doing such a ride a few years ago, but I really loved spending hours on my bike travelling up and down between towns, staying in old pubs because they were cheap. It was a grand way to get around and it was never dull.

On another trip, I stayed a night in Narrabri. I had stayed there before but this time my room might have been one of the worst rooms in the country. The furniture was shabby and, unlike most pub rooms, it had never been elegant, even when it was new.

There were missing drawers, and broken handles, and there was an ugly and broken sink jutting out into the lower bunk.

There were long legged spiders in the corners of the ceiling, and the curtain was clumped into a corner and hanging half off its track. The towels were old and frayed, and there was paint coming off the ceiling and furnishings. The fan was cracked and old and the switch was only accessible from the top bunk.

Outside my window, I had a close up view of a cell phone tower and the hallway smelled damp. It was no better in the sad damp bathroom.

I knew they had better rooms but it never occurred to me to complain. As long as the bed was clean and I could sleep, I did not mind at all. I was on a road trip on my motorbike and it was all part of the adventure.

***

The next day I rode from Narrabri to Moree. It was over a hundred kilometres of the flattest landscape I had ever seen. I could see across to the horizon in the distance.

This was quite a novelty for me because in New Zealand I had been surrounded by hills most of my life and I had only seen the horizon when looking across the ocean. It felt like I was on the edge of the wide flat open spaces of the Australian Outback. Perhaps I was.

A road sign just out of Moree suggested I should look out for Kangaroos for the next 120 kilometres, so I did. I had seen a few in my travels but the majority seem to live on the golf courses. They have terrible road skills and are often hit by cars.

I once watched a kangaroo jump out next to my car and then leap on and off the road in front of me as if it had a death wish.

Crows on the other hand are smart road users. If they are on the road when I approach, they casually walk out of my way in a dignified manner or bounce along using wing assisted hopping. I have never seen a flattened crow.

On this trip, a crow moved just over the line into the other lane and waited there for me to pass. It looked like he was laughing.

I saw two emus bouncing along in the long grassy field by the road and was excited. This was my first and only sighting of emus outside a zoo.

I spent the middle part of the trip observing the large number of pieces of black tyre rubber on the road verge. I estimated there were between one and two exploded tyres for every kilometre I travelled.

This worried me, as a motorbike has only two tyres and could not afford to lose either. I consoled myself by assuming the burst tires came from big rigs with eighteen wheels and plenty of back-ups.

I was reassured to see a cell phone tower miles from any sign of civilisation. Cell phone coverage was unreliable along the trip so I decided that if I broke down, I would have to break down right there. Roadside rescue would only be useful if I could call them.

I spent the last part of the trip studying the signs of damage on the road. In places, the heat had melted the road and the white lines had lifted and become wavy. In others, the middle of the road had risen up and created a giant pimple that buckled the road and made the bike jump.

I spent many miles looking for the perfect spot to stop and take a photo of a road pimple or a wavy line but the sides of the road were narrow. I didn't get the photo I wanted but looking for one kept me busy for a large part of the trip.

I found the road signs interesting too. There were community advisory signs that said things like "Take a Break" or "Revive and Survive," and as I crossed the border from New South Wales into Queensland, the messages got more serious. They carried messages like "Rest or R.I.P." and "Every K over is a killer," or the cheery "Tired drivers die."

I was already feeling bombarded with the tragic possibilities of not getting enough rest when I came across an electronic sign that spoke to me personally. "Your speed is 97km's. Take a break now."

The road authorities had also made an effort to make sure we noticed every curve in the road. I counted fifteen arrows on a longish corner and a kaleidoscopic group of about twenty red warning signs and yellow cautions signs on both sides of a curve on the Cunningham highway. The corner was not that bad. The driveway on my home in New Zealand is worse.

I could tell I was coming up to a town by the fast food signs that sprang up out of the ground like huge, flat, and colourful mushrooms. Sometimes they surprised me.

On a remote windy piece of road I could not miss a huge sign with the big yellow "M" that said, "Your next McDonalds is only 75 minutes away." Later, there was another sign, "Your next McDonalds is only 55 minutes away."

Are there really people who plan their travel around the next McDonalds? Is there a group of travellers who spend their time wondering where their next all meat patty, special sauce, pickles, cheese and onions on a sesame seed bun is going to come from?

Do we have to know about it hours before we get there?

In any case, I prefer to try local specialties like the strange grey seafood soup with the odd name I cannot recall, that I tried in Tasmania. It was delicious.

Then there was the chicken Laksa I ordered one night from an Asian noodle house. Along with the chicken and vegetables, it had some interesting cubes of rubbery stuff that may have been dried tofu, or possibly offcuts from a rubber boot factory. Now that is not just dinner. That is an adventure.

***

Back in Queensland, my little yellow motorbike developed a terrible rattle.

I made heads turn by riding into town on what sounded like a concrete drill and people were even more surprised when I took off my helmet and revealed my age.

Technically, I have always been a grandma on a bike, but I started to feel every year of my age. I was riding my motorbike in the slow lanes of the motorway and pushbikes were overtaking.

I knew something was wrong with the bike. It was kind of chugging along like an old lawn mower and when I stopped, the engine seemed almost hot enough to produce steam.

One day the chain caught on something, the wheels

abruptly stopped turning, and the bike skidded to a halt. Luckily, I was in a small side street and not going fast

RACQ came with their enormous truck (I was so glad to have roadside assistance) but they did not have the straps they needed to secure the bike. They had to send for a second truck.

People driving by must have wondered what kind of tragic accident needed two big breakdown trucks. Not that small bike surely.

The second truck managed to secure my little bike in the middle of its huge tray, and the driver took us both home.

It had only been a few weeks since the same company had rescued me from a hot motorway exit when my battery terminals came loose. I should have been getting frequent flyer miles.

After talking to Phil, I had another go at tightening the chain. I thought the chain was fine, but what did I know? I had only been riding a bike for five months and I never intended to be a mechanic.

After the chain failure, I rode my bike even slower, bracing myself for a sudden stop and a quick flight over the handlebars. Finally, I found a local mechanic and took my bike in for some much-needed repairs.

The mechanic tightened the chain correctly, ordered a new water pump, and took the last of my small stash of money. I felt a little more confident on the bike so I headed back on another two-day trip to Mudgee so Phil could look at my bike.

On one of the longest stretches of road and twelve kilometres from the nearest town, my bike stopped working. I checked the petrol and there was still enough to swish around the tank. I checked the battery connections; because that was the only thing I knew how to check. Everything seemed fine.

I tried to ring Phil, but there was no phone signal. This did not surprise me. It was a remote spot, and not the one with the cell phone tower.

I stared at the bike for some time and up and down the quiet road, hoping for a miracle. Finally, I remembered the mechanic had turned off the reserve petrol tank when he was working on the bike. By flicking the switch back, I got the bike to acknowledge the reserve tank of petrol and I was back on the road again, crisis over.

Then a little red light came on. It meant the motor was overheating. I still had forty kilometres to go to the next town so I said a quick prayer, slowed down to about fifty and babied my bike the rest of the way.

I was surprised to find it was a town with a motorbike shop, and even better, they agreed to look at my bike almost immediately. Just over an hour and just under a hundred dollars later, they sent me on my way with a new radiator cap and a fan that was rigged to work continuously.

Twenty minutes later, in the middle of nowhere, there was a large hot explosion on my leg. Bizarrely, my first thought was that I had somehow been splattered with my own warm blood.

When I stopped the bike, I realised that the plastic cap had blown off the coolant tank and my jeans leg was covered with sticky green coolant.

There are times when it is a real advantage that I am not fazed by a little mess.

There was no way I would find the cap in the long grass so I stood looking at my bike helplessly.

Two bikers held their thumbs up as they went past. This is the national signal for "Are you alright?" I was not, so I signalled thumbs down. Rather reluctantly, they pulled over and stopped. They suggested I cover the coolant tank outlet with something, so I found a piece of junk plastic and tied it on with an old pair of socks.

Then I set off on another slow trip, limping toward town, while trucks I had passed earlier in the day swerved impatiently around me.

Luckily, I was stopping at the next town for the night anyway and even better, a phone call to Phil meant I was able to make some minor repairs myself. I refilled the coolant tank and was back on the road in the morning. It was so good to reach Mudgee.

Despite Phil's heroic efforts on my behalf, my bike did not recover. When Phil opened the engine head, he opened a can of worms. Someone had used dodgy bolts and they were not holding properly.

That explained why the bike was leaking in the first place, and why, after I had done nine thousand kilometres, it had finally keeled over and refused to go any further.

I was lucky the bike made it as far as it did.

After that, my bike was off the road and I was enviously watching the bikers ride past.

Just one year earlier, I would never have dreamed of owning a motorbike. Now, I did not know how I would manage without it.

Trains, Cars, and Pushbikes

My first housesit without the motorbike was out in a beautiful country region that would have been fun to explore on my bike.

Instead I had to make do with a pushbike.

I was very lucky to have it because it was five kilometres to the nearest shops, and further than that to a library or a train station.

One afternoon, I went out on a ride to town to post some mail, buy some groceries, and use the Internet at the information centre. It was about five kilometres to town and all up and down hills.

By the first hill, I was already tired and within five minutes, I was off the bike and walking.

I had just lost my only income so I was living very frugally. I had not had a haircut in six months and my hair was long, blond, and shapeless apart from a two-inch strip of mousy brown and grey where the dye was growing out.

I was wearing the clothes I wore the day before to save washing, and my only shoes were now grey with tears in the fabric. There were scratches on my arms from hunting in the bushes for geocaches, and I had itchy red eyes that had not responded to eye drops.

One of the things I like about being my age is that I am much less concerned with what people think of me, but even so, I was glad I was not likely to meet anyone I knew this far out of town.

I was not very fit, so I was riding as if I was in some sort of bizarre triathlon, where the downhill was a bike ride and the uphill was a slow walk. Thirty minutes later I was hot, tired, and although I did not know it at the time, I was stressed.

I had called ahead, but getting my computer online still proved tricky for the two women at the centre who thought that if I plugged in my laptop, it might overload their system and blow up the building. After some discussion, I finally settled into the middle seat at the computer desk.

I was looking forward to catching up on over a hundred emails that had arrived since I was last online and to following up on the other internet tasks that I usually had all day to do. First, one of the women came over to talk and then the other woman started to do some photocopying on the machine on the other side of me.

Next, a teenage boy arrived and began to talk across me to his mum, who was still noisily photocopying right next to my ear. I was piggy in the middle and I had trouble concentrating while the mother kept talking across me and telling her son how much he smelled and that he should buy deodorant.

It was all a bit much, so I told the woman I did not notice any smell but the noise of the photocopier was annoying. The woman left and within minutes, a bearded man came over to tell me that when staff need to use the photocopier, they have priority.

I was embarrassed and annoyed and I acted in my usual calm and collected manner. I insisted I did not tell her to stop and then dissolved into tears of frustration.

The man was apologetic and the women were concerned. I tried to insist I was fine but it was quite obvious I was not, so I got to use the computer alone while the staff huddled in the office to discuss the situation and probably for safety. I expect they were also wondering which loony bin I had escaped from.

At least it kept the noisy woman away while I did the most urgent things I needed to, and after a bit of public relations work and apologies all around, I left hoping that it would be okay to return.

At the grocery store, I was still feeling very sorry for myself. I had very little money but I made good use of it. I bought green vegetables for health and well-being and chocolate biscuits and sarsaparilla for my soul.

On my way home, I was so proud of myself. I stayed on the bike longer and cycled up some of the shorter inclines, even though I was bent over under the weight of a backpack full to bursting with a few essential groceries. I also had a shopping bag slung beneath the cross bar of my too big boys bike. It kept getting in the way as I pedalled, giving me a bandy look with my knees out wide.

There were no footpaths on the country road, and the edge of the road was mostly gravel and a slippery scary place. I stuck as close as I could to the edge, and cars tended to give me a wide berth.

I did my best to look competent and in control as I walked up the hills so people would not stop and ask if I was alright. I loved the downhill runs and I picked up a bit of speed. With the wind in my hair, it reminded me ever so slightly of motorbike riding. It was a small thrill, especially as there was an element of risk.

I had the world's noisiest bike brakes and they sounded quite similar to truck engine breaks. I was reluctant to use them in a built up area. If I had to stop in a hurry, I might have had to jump ship and let the bike go.

I got home just as the sun faded into its usual beautiful golden orange glow along the horizon, and taking off the backpack of groceries was like removing an anvil from my shoulders. I felt light enough to float.

For a poor, non-domestic type, single woman, dinner was awesome. I had my vegetables with chicken, and followed it with a homemade apple crumble I had made earlier in the day. I also had the complete packet of chocolate biscuits and two glasses of fizzy.

After all that, I was feeling much better, but only until Phil called. He said he had made peanut butter on toast for his dinner. Now I was feeling guilty again. I wish I had been there to make him dinner.

I hoped the next day would be less stressful. I could not afford to use the chocolate biscuit prescription too often.

I spent the last of the daylight feeding the dog and the pony and, as it had not rained since I arrived, giving the garden a good soaking.

It rained for the next two days.

***

I am a compulsive explorer, so when the weather cleared, I decided to visit a town about fifteen kilometres away. There were no buses, so I chose the only option available and took the pedal bike.

The road in was tiring and long. It was mostly steep roller coaster hills, so I decided to go home another way.

It turned out to be worse. What looked so flat on the map, turned out to be a series of even bigger switchback hills. I could have got a nosebleed up there.

The fifteen kilometres turned into more than

twenty, with twists, turns, and steep inclines. I walked up most of the hills. After one particularly steep hill, I realised I would have to walk down as well. It was so steep, that with my dodgy noisy brakes, I could either hit the brakes and deafen the locals, or hit the bottom at one hundred kilometres an hour.

I chose to live.

There were some magnificent views across the hills and the journey was an adventure, but I was so worn out when I got home that I could hardly stand.

***

My next house sit was in a Brisbane suburb. It was a relief to have trains, buses, and ferries, all within walking distance. They were a cheap option for getting around, and could also provide much entertainment.

One night I was in a train carriage between a group of four young girls that were dressed in skimpy maid uniforms and more than a dozen young males who were all hyped up trying to impress the girls.

From my seat, I could only see the boys and they were hilarious. They preened and boasted to each other and puffed put their chests. A group of four were actually dancing, their eyes on the blackened mirror windows, and their minds on the girls they hoped were watching.

Most of us "old" people in between the two groups were head down pretending not to notice but I was enjoying the antics of the boys. I could watch all I liked because in their current state I was invisible.

The boys complained loudly because they were not going to the same party as the girls, but they all got off at the same station anyway. It was my station and I was right in the middle of the two groups.

As I got up to leave, I locked eyes with the woman across from me and she gave me a pitying smile. I smiled back and bravely attached myself to the group of hyped up youths standing by the door. I took a quick look down the other end of the carriage and noticed that the girls were now hanging from the overhead straps so that their dresses rode up to obscene levels.

As we stepped off the train, the gang of young boys magically parted like the red sea to let me through. I expect I was blocking their view.

At times like that, I am glad I never had daughters. From the way the girls left the train and ran across the road, screaming and waving their hands in the air, it was obvious they were already tanked up and it was only 6pm. Their party had not even started yet.

I saw part of a documentary once about the violence on Queensland trains. Now that I was travelling by train, I was starting to see a new side to Brisbane, especially after dark.

One day there were hooligans in the rear section of the carriage intimidating people in nearby seats. On another, a middle-aged woman sprawled across a station seat while four police officers tried to hold a meaningful conversation with her.

A young man on a daytime train came closer to talk to a friend near me and told him that he had $75,000 in fines for fighting on the train. He had another $16,000 for other offences and expected to go to jail soon. He seemed particularly proud of this.

I had my own reputation for causing trouble on the train.

***

I was on my way to a free concert and travelling on

a busy early evening train with lots of people on their way home from work.

Most of the passengers were smartly dressed professional looking people and I was in my usual jeans and sneakers. There were other people there wearing jeans, but they had accessorised them with fancy bags with significant labels and funky shoes. I clutched my year old backpack to my chest and wondered if I would ever even own a handbag, let alone a Gucci.

Like most people, I had worked that day, but unlike most people, my work took less than an hour and I spent the rest of the day exploring the city.

Most of those people probably made more in an hour than I did in a week but they looked so serious and formal.

I earned twenty dollars for my work and had to wait four weeks for payment, but I was quite satisfied with that, considering the trade-off in extra time. While they were bound to an office or a boss, I was free to do as I pleased.

There was a young man sitting diagonally opposite me who began to doze off and lapse into a deep upright coma-like sleep. I worried that he might miss his station and wondered if I should wake him.

After we had travelled through a few stations this way, he opened his bloodshot eyes and looked blearily around in the way that people sometimes do when they are not quite awake.

He looked at me. I was watching him and trying to work out if he was awake enough to know where he was or if I should tell him. Suddenly he stood up and left.

I assumed that despite his still stunned and half-awake appearance he had recognised his station. Instead, he moved along the carriage to another seat that was as far away from me as possible.

I felt like a train stalker.

***

A few months later, I was staying in Brisbane city again and back on a yellow bike, but it was not my yellow bike.

My motorbike was still off the road. I had been using the trains and buses, but I remembered the pushbike I rode in the country. It had helped me become fitter and build up my stamina. I decided to try bike riding again.

This bike was the best of three that were in the shed. It was a little rusty and the tires were low but at least it worked. It was set up for the tall young man who usually used it. The seat was so high that to ride it I had to lean over in a racing pose as if I was doing the Tour de France.

My bike helmet was also too big and very dusty. I took it off to retract the strap and removed a small spider that I had not noticed before.

The numbers on the gears were so worn I could not read them, so I wobbled off in the wrong gear for a few minutes while passers-by wondered why someone with my lack of bike skills was riding at all.

Finally, I was flying down the hill and it was almost like being back on my motorbike. It was so good to be out on the road again.

Then I changed gears to go up the hill and I lost traction completely, spinning the pedals uselessly for a minute before coming to an ungraceful stop at the side of the road.

It seemed I was destined to walk uphills again. At the top, I reset the gears and started again. After half an hour of stop start riding, I worked out that if I stayed within just two or three gears I was fine.

My first stop was a gas station to put some air into the tires. After circling the petrol station several times, I found the air filler-upper between the pumps and tried to look competent as I fiddled with the machine.

Suddenly, a large spider appeared from somewhere inside the rusty bike handle bars.

He was quite chunky and big enough to take up most of the palm of my hand. I could not work out where he had been hidden. He must have been the Houdini of all spiders.

A couple of flicks and he was off the handlebars and on the concrete running for the nearest tall thing he could climb. That would be me.

I did a quick sidestep and he headed off onto the tarmac while I quickly headed off to my next adventure.

***

One weekend I had a car to use. My son had gone to Melbourne and had kindly left his car with me for the weekend. I made plans to visit my family and maybe take my youngest son somewhere nice. As I dropped my boy off at the airport, I found there was almost no petrol in the car and neither of us had money to buy some.

I had not had an income since I had to stop my online job. My finances were in a pitiful state and I had only the cash in my wallet. I could not afford petrol so I had to put off my plans for family visits.

The car had a damaged window that was held up with masking tape. My son warned me that, if the weather was hot, the window might come unstuck and fall down again.

Heat was the least of my worries that weekend.

After the rain soaked through everything for the whole day, the tape gave way and the window was at half-mast all night.

I did my best to cover the window with a couple of plastic shopping bags that I had ripped to fit.

It looked shockingly awful but went quite well with the old McDonalds packets he had used to decorate the rear floor of the car.

On Sunday, it rained again and I was grateful to have the car so I did not have to walk to church. I parked around the corner so as not to panic the nice people at church who had just met me.

Bless the people of Mitchelton for being so honest. I worried about the car sitting outside with the window wide open for three hours but it was still there on my return. There are suburbs and there are suburbs. This seemed to be a good one.

When I picked up my son from the airport, the car was now on critically empty. Mother of the year here I come.

Packing Light

Moving into someone's home as a house sitter is not like going to a motel. You will have the use of a fully stocked kitchen, laundry, and living area. If the homeowners are agreeable, you will probably also have the use of a library of books and videos.

This makes packing light easy.

Most things you need will be in the home. Everything from cooking pots to a clothes iron and house cleaning equipment will come with the house, so there is not much to worry about. If there is anything else you really must have, perhaps a hair dryer, then you could ask before you arrive or bring your own.

When I moved into my first house sit, I took only what I could carry in my backpack and the small bag on the front of my motorbike.

I took clothes, toiletries, and not much else. I still don't take things like laundry powder or dishwashing liquid as I can buy it when I get there. If it is a long house sit, I will probably use what is there and replace it during my stay.

Because I do not have to dress for work or even social outings, I can afford to carry fewer clothes than most people would need. The warm climate means I do not need any bulky jackets and the internet has replaced all my reference books and even reading books.

If you might be doing a lot of house sitting, get

some good strong bags or suitcases that will be convenient to use. It can be very hard to find things in a large deep bag, and depending on how long your stay is, you might be living out of those cases, so make sure they are practical.

After I had been doing house sitting for a while, I bought some cheap plastic drawers that could be disassembled for packing. They only lasted about a year but they kept my things off the floor and tidied away quite nicely.

Below is a list of things I suggest you take with you if you are travelling light.

1. Two pairs of jeans or long pants
2. Two pairs of shorts, skirts or dresses
3. Four short-sleeved tops and two long sleeved
4. Underwear and socks for 5-7 days
5. Swimming costume
6. Hairbrush, nail clippers, tweezers
7. Toilet needs, toothbrush, soap etc. Moisturiser
8. One or two small towels that dry easily
9. A small first aid kit including pain killers, throat lozenges or necessary medications
10. A compact sewing kit
11. An umbrella or raincoat
12. A small torch and batteries (I found a head torch was a practical option)
13. Cell phone and charger
14. A small amount of cash in case there are no card facilities or for purchasing at a market or roadside stall
15. Emergency food and water (On the bike this is just a muesli bar and one bottle of water)
16. A simple tool kit, depending on your mode of transport

17. A camera (Optional)
18. A laptop. (Optional)
19. A warm jacket (Depending on the weather)

Of course your needs may be different, especially if you are travelling in a car or a campervan.

I found that packing light was part of the adventure. By leaving most of my possessions behind, I left many of my worries behind. There is an incredible sense of freedom in owning and carrying very little.

After I began to travel in a station wagon instead of on my motorbike, I began to accumulate other items that seemed necessary.

I now have far more than the two bags that I started with but far less than most people. Moving house forces me to re-evaluate my possessions and consider whether I truly need the things I own. I pare down each time I shift. I have a regular clean out and discard anything that is not useful or beautiful.

Having so few possessions to worry about is liberating. I have not much of my own to polish, repair, repaint, or renovate. It is so much like being on permanent holiday.

One item that is important to me is my laptop computer. Although there are computers and internet access in many homes and at every library, I always travel with my laptop. If I had to choose again, I would buy one that was a little lighter than the one that I have now, but I will not travel without it.

It has my contact details, my schedule, my photos and of course my notes about my trip. It is my phone book, my job finder and a source of useful maps. I am also a writer and need a full sized keyboard. A smaller alternative that would work for most people would be a computer enabled phone or a tablet like the iPad.

When I had the use of a car, my first big purchase was a printer, to go with the laptop. It was another generous gift from Phil. I use it to print out local maps for geocaching, letters home, to do lists, and copies of my writing to check. It is big and bulky but it is important to me because I am a writer.

Most homes I stay in have printers, but perhaps because mine is so personal to me, I feel it is an imposition to use them, even when they have been offered. Printers can be temperamental and are easy to damage or jam when you are not familiar with them.

A few other items I carry now that I have the car are some snorkelling gear and a boogie board. I am often near the beach so these are cheap fun.

I have more notebooks, clothes, shoes, and a file for important papers. I also carry a small amount of emergency food and my juicer. It is an indulgence but I love fresh juice and it is healthy.

I try to continue to travel light, but it is so easy to get back into old habits and accumulate too many things.

When I first started house sitting, I could leave at almost a moment's notice. The last time I shifted, it took several hours. Most of that time I was sorting and discarding, and I still had five bags to carry plus some items Phil had left with me.

I recommend that you take as little as possible to make it easy on yourself.

In New Zealand, I used to live in a house with five bedrooms and three living rooms, and there was never enough storage room. Items seemed to accumulate exponentially. We began to overflow the storage spaces with old suitcases, puzzles, craft materials, and schoolbooks we couldn't bear to part with.

Most people that house sit will have some items in

storage. I have cold weather clothes and blankets stashed in New Zealand, items for my own house stored in Sydney, and books in both places.

Although I have tried to cut down on every unnecessary possession, I love books and have found it hard to discard them.

I have a large library of self-improvement books. Some of them have given me the confidence and motivation to set goals and to go after them and I don't want to sell them yet. If you can leave some of your "things" behind, you might find you don't miss them after all.

Because I do not have many clothes, I only buy items that are comfortable and make me feel good. I try to buy clothes that fit well and that are a good colour for me. It might take a bit longer to find the right clothes at cheap prices, but it is nice to feel good about myself, even on a small budget.

Second-hand shops have been my main source of clothes but they vary in quality and price. Find the right one and you can get everything you need. I look out for local sales too. In Goondiwindi, I bought new tops for less than the price of second-hand ones in Maleny. Having so much free time means I can comparison shop and find bargains

I like clothes that are easy care and that dry quickly. I wear a lot of cotton, so I take care when washing not to leave things to crease in the machine and fold them as soon as they are dry. I hardly ever need to iron.

I spend a lot of time walking and exploring, so good shoes are more important than good clothes. After spending one day in bad shoes that left me with ugly and painful blisters, I spent extra to get the best quality running shoes from a factory outlet and added quality inserts. I also wear sandals a lot when it is hot. They cost very little but the rubber soles are kind on my feet.

I do not have many accessories, but a hat can make a hot walk more comfortable and an umbrella can make a walk in the rain a fun event instead of a chore. I have the hat and can usually wait out the rain.

People who know me would laugh to see me giving out clothes advice or beauty tips. I neglect my eyebrows until they are straggly and sometimes bite the skin around my nails quite ragged, but I have learned a few things in my travels about beauty on the road especially when money is tight.

Keep it simple. I always have a good moisturiser and use it daily. Cleansers and toners are nice to have but not essential. As long as you do not wash your face with soap or chemicals then I find a moisturiser is enough. Do not forget your neck. It gets dry too.

If you have light skin you will probably benefit from a moisturiser with sunscreen, but I am wary of the chemicals and prefer not to apply them to my face. I use a hat instead.

Pare down the makeup. If you are camping or going bush then you might not need to take any at all. If you want to dress up sometimes all you need is the one lipstick that flatters your skin colour, mascara in black or black/brown depending on your colouring, and one of the new compacts that is a foundation, a blush and eye shadow all in one. Keep it in a padded and secure bag to minimise any mess if the powder leaks in your bag. A plastic zip lock bag is ideal. Your moisturiser can be used as a make-up remover.

Take a kit with nail clippers, tweezers, and small scissors corralled into a handy bag. Depending on your travel plans, you might also like to take a small magnifying mirror. Having regular days for nail and eyebrow care can avoid the sinking feeling I get when I am out on the town and realise that I have done neither lately.

If you are as attractive to mosquitos as I am, then a good repellent and an anti-itch cream might be important. Every time I return to Queensland after some time away, I get itchy bites that I cannot avoid scratching until I have red blotches all over my legs. It is not attractive.

If you are going to be travelling anywhere on a plane, keep in mind the restrictions. Currently you cannot take any liquids over 100mls on some flights. I fly between New Zealand and Australia often so I usually have a small tube of toothpaste just for travelling.

A simple and compact sewing repair kit, first aid kit and a medicine kit can all be useful. You do not want to find yourself out of painkiller when you have a headache in the middle of the night, or with a sagging hem when you are three weeks from your home sewing machine. You know what you will use. Most of it can be bought if you need it so do not stress. I have never had a sewing kit or a first aid kit, although I have found a packet of Panadol useful sometimes.

Travelling should be fun, so it is up to you what to take. If you need your tennis gear, your cello or your favourite “World’s Best Mum” mug, then that is up to you. As long as you can pack it and carry it, anything is possible.

Ups and Downs

Some days, not having a home of my own, and being always on the move can be tiring. I wonder if I am doing the right thing. I miss my family and I wish I had more money to call them. Sometimes, I would like more money for a haircut or to recolour my hair.

I have even found myself looking longingly at a pile of hot chips left over on someone's plate, or drooling over a beautifully displayed platter of some delicious lunch that I did not have enough money to buy.

Those days can happen anywhere. When I am feeling unmotivated and uninspired, the best thing to do is to make some new plans.

When I miss my family, I call them or make plans to visit them.

When I feel the lack of money, I consider whether I want to go back and get a job or whether I could do something else to make money for a bit. Perhaps I could get a part-time job or do some freelance work. There were always options.

I think back to the time when I was raising my six sons and my then husband was hardly ever at home to help. I chose to be a stay at home mother and I loved that time of my life, but I had discouraging times then too. It happens anywhere.

When I feel dowdy, I choose something I can change and work on that. I go out for a walk, do some exercises, or just tie my hair up into a ponytail.

Sometimes I even allow myself an afternoon nap or get myself something nice that I can afford like an ice cream.

Every time I reconsider my options, I remember how much I love being on the road and how much I hated reporting to unfair and uninspiring bosses. I chose freedom and adventure. I am so lucky. This is my dream and I am living it.

Being a full-time house sitter is a marvellous profession, and I love it, but there are a few disadvantages. Being a vagabond with no fixed abode is one of them, and it can cause a few problems.

I was surprised by how often I needed to provide an address, even without utility bills. There are the insurance companies, roadside rescue and of course, friends and family who want to know where to post me a letter or birthday card. I prefer not to give out my temporary addresses because I do not want the family I am house sitting for to have mail to forward when I leave.

I have overcome this by setting up a Post Office box. I share it with Phil who now works one week in a mine in Western Australia and often stays with me the other week. We chose one near the airport as it is the one place we can count on visiting regularly. It is an easy and obvious option that provides continuity.

The other thing I really miss is the opportunity to be more financially supportive to my sons.

Most of them are students and could use some help. I think that a little scrimping will not do them any harm, but I wish I had more money for family birthdays and to help out when times are tough. My gifts are sometimes extremely inexpensive, depending on my situation at the time.

On the day of my sons twenty fourth birthday, I

bought him a pair of wind up chattering teeth.

I put them in a happy birthday box I got for one dollar fifty along with a plastic celebration glass with flashing coloured lights and some chocolate. All up, it cost just over ten dollars.

He was not overwhelmed but he did smile. He is a wonderful son and deserves more.

It was a low point for me. I do not mind spending so little on myself but I feel bad being so stingy with my boys. I used some more of my precious money to buy a few treats and, along with food he bought himself, we made a special dinner and I reminded myself that some things are more important than money.

It may only be a ten-dollar birthday, but I am sure it was a much better day for me and my family than it was for the people who live in developing countries and made the items I bought. It is such a privilege to live in Australia. I love it here.

You do not need money to make life fun and interesting. Happiness comes from being with friends and family and making the best of what you have.

That evening, my oldest son and his family came over with some cousins and we celebrated together. The important things in life are not money, but family and friends. I have both in large numbers. I am happy, healthy, and safe.

My problems have been minor and my good fortune has been major. I live in a country and at a time when I have so many options. I can live in a mansion or a tent. I can ride a motorbike or a camel. I can stay at home or travel around the world if I want. The world is filled with wonderful, beautiful options.

By careful shopping, I can have all sorts of goodies. For just a few dollars, I can have yoghurt for breakfast and toasted sandwiches for lunch. It is amazing how good everything tastes and how much I appreciate the simple things in life now that I am living so simply.

A banana has such a wonderful sweetness and a carrot has become an acceptable snack, but I also have chocolate chip biscuits sometimes. Some days, they are such a good price I just have to buy them.

That is the secret of my wonderful life really. I eat healthy most of the time and enjoy a treat sometimes.

I have wonderful adventures and fun most days, but when things go wrong, I just move on.

Years End

On Christmas Day, Phil was working so I stayed home in my pyjamas.

One of my sons had invited me to the family gathering they were having with their dads' relations. I get on well with them but I was intimidated by my sisters-in-law's cooking. They have made the same dishes for every family gathering I have ever been to and have perfected the art.

Chop Suey, barbecue, potato salad, raw fish floating in a soup of cucumber, onions, tomatoes and coconut milk, and grey taro cooked in grey sauce made from onions and more coconut milk. In recent years, they have become more creative but they still have a natural flare for making tasty dishes.

I can cook beautifully, but only one time out of four, so it is touch and go whether anything I make will be delicious, bland, or a disaster.

I played it safe and planned a platter of cheese and pineapple sticks, chips, grapes, apricot balls and little spicy sausages I knew my boys would like.

On Christmas morning, I spent all morning thinking about putting the platter together and mentally preparing for the gathering with my ex's family. Then I stayed home.

It was a very wet day. The rain was falling as if the heavens were being emptied for a spring clean. As it got later and later, the idea of crashing my ex's family for

Christmas dinner became less and less appealing until I gave away the idea entirely and rejoiced in the relaxed freedom of being alone and single. I read books, watched TV, played on Facebook, and stayed in my pyjamas all morning.

Then there was a knock on the door. After a quick frantic chase around the house, I grabbed some crinkled shorts and a t-shirt.

It was two of my sons.

I was so happy to see them that I spent the next ten minutes offering them things from my stash of Christmas goodies; juice, spicy sausage, cheese and pineapple, corn chips and dip, thick hot chocolate. Then I ate most of it myself while they watched TV and opened their gifts from me.

They showed a heartening appreciation for my modest, but well thought out, gifts and then my youngest insisted he wanted to swim and he did not want to swim alone.

It was still raining, but I was just happy to spend the time with my son that I decided to brave the tempest. We splashed and cavorted in the overflowing pool under the patter of heavy rain.

It was amazing watching the raindrops bounce up to six inches off the surface of the water from underneath. I wished I had a waterproof camera. The neighbours probably wish they had some peace and quiet.

As my son jumped, flipped, and crashed, in the too full pool, there was much laughter and splashing. The water tossed and heaved like an ocean storm. It was a crazy way to spend Christmas but so much fun.

The year was almost at an end and I realised I was well satisfied with my life. My goals for the year were to have fun, to discover, to explore, and to find adventure.

I had been living my dream.

In some ways, it was a year of two distinct parts; the wild adventurous motorbike rider, and the staid mother of six and grandmother of three. I have straddled the two worlds as my family tried to cope with my new life and my gypsy lifestyle.

I am a great believer in experiences. I think far too many people get to the end of life and regret the things they did not do. If you have a dream, follow it. If you have a passion, enjoy it. Get involved and try something new each day.

Life is good. I have spent a wonderful year having adventures and finding new horizons and I have a thirst for more adventure. Ordinary is not in my vocabulary any more.

Sometimes family, and even close friends, do not understand. It seems frivolous, or unfair, or just too good to be true.

Sometimes it even seems a bit frivolous to me, like a permanent holiday. My life used to revolve around the care of six sons and at the same time, I was always involved in a range of voluntary projects.

Now I have up to twelve hours a day to use as I choose.

I have used some of that time to help with short community projects. I helped set up for a community festival, visited a lady in a hospital far from her friends, joined a beach clean-up after the floods, and helped disabled children experience sailing.

I would like to do more.

One day I might devote much more time to a charitable cause, or, I might sail the Greek Islands on Phil's yacht.

Nothing has to be forever. It is worth being brave and setting out on an adventure that interests you.

In many ways I consider this my sabbatical year. The year I have sat back, examined my life, and realised who I am, what I value, and what I enjoy. After being a full-time mum for so many years, it has been satisfying, and a little odd, to be both on my own and have so much freedom. I believe I am a better person for taking this time.

If you have a dream, I encourage you to trust your instincts.

Try that new recipe, take that new course, hug a child, call a friend, or take a year-long holiday. If you are ready for something more, you might even consider living on the road for a while. Life is full of opportunity so do not miss out.

Phil and I sometimes marvel at how things have come together. We wonder what part Josh, the raging alcoholic, had to play in our lives. If he had not sent the letter to my work, I suspect I might not have been made redundant.

If my boss had been supportive, I might have stayed at work. If my ex had not left for Australia taking my youngest I would almost certainly have stayed in New Zealand. If, if, if ......

Life is so amazing. There is a network of small-interconnected actions that each leads us on to our destination in life. Each movement, each decision, each glance, even each thought, changes things forever, and leads us on to our future.

Out of all the hundreds of women online, Phil picked me to "smile" at. I could so easily have missed meeting the one person in this world who really seems suited to me. He knows what I like sometimes before I do.

I have been known to spend twenty minutes choosing socks and weeks looking for just the right shoes. I ask his advice and he chooses just what I know I would have chosen if I had been given another four hours to think about it.

Phil is generous, loving, talented, smart, and kind to small children and animals. More importantly for me he is reliable. After missing this for so long, it is so relaxing to be able to trust someone as I do him. I no longer have to second-guess every move or have back up plans for every event.

Recently my ex-husband finally accepted the inevitability of divorce and is now working on making it legal. This coming year might just be the year to bring my two lives together. The year when my sons accept my new relationship and we become one big, tangled but comfortable family.

I look back on the goal list I made a few years ago after I left my marriage.

I wanted a man I could love, trust and admire. I wanted an income and a useful job. I wished for more travel, a nice home, and time with family.

I have spent time with family. I have lived in many nice homes, and I sure have travelled. I have my own yellow motorbike and shares in a yacht, both passports to more adventure.

I have Phil; my awesome Aussie boyfriend who is teaching me how to really love someone, how to accept love and who inspires me to want to be a better person.

I have laughed more over this last year than I did in the last twenty years combined, and I have a constant smile in my heart. I have a completely new life that I love, and I know one thing for sure. There are many more adventures to come; I will make sure of that.

To keep reading
and see what adventures
Nikki is having now,
visit her blog, at

www.travellerinoz.blogspot.com

Useful Websites

Housesitting and working in Australia

www.aussiehousesitters.com.au

Aussie House Sitters specialise in housesitting jobs within Australia. They are cheaper than other sites I considered and allow you to apply for positions all over the country for the one fee.

You can scroll through the homeowner ads or leave your profile, complete with a photograph, and let homeowners contact you.

Once registered, Aussie House Sitters also offer a house sitting agreement you can change to suit your needs.

This is the only site I have used and I have had a successful year of almost constant housesitting. I recommend it.

www.housecarers.com.au

This is another nice site to find house sits. I have not used it but I can see it has housesitting jobs in other countries. This could be an advantage if you plan to travel further afield.

www.jobsearch.gov.au

This government website is a good place to start looking for all types of employment, from full time to seasonal. It also has links to other employment websites.

Immigration

www.immi.gov.au

Information and advice about immigrating to Australia

Travelling in Australia

Australia is an amazing country to explore and there is so much variety, from sunny beaches, to snowy mountains, and the vast and remote sunburned outback

In my travels so far, I have just scratched the surface of the possible adventures to be had here. For more information about travel, accommodation and attractions, visit one of the following websites.

Australian Travel Guide

www.australiaeguide.com.au

This site covers everything from arrivals to departures and everything in between. It has information about transport, accommodation, and attractions. You will find it very useful, even if you are an Australian.

International Travel Guide

www.traveleguides.com

The same website as above has comprehensive travel information and guides to every country from Afghanistan to Yemen. Start your next adventure here.

About the Author

Nikki Ah Wong is the 50-year-old mother of six sons and grandmother of four. A few years ago, she was a well-paid manager for a national childcare organization in New Zealand and managed up to 120 people. Today she has no fixed income, no fixed address and lives on less than the minimum wage.

Nikki describes herself as an explorer and a wonder aficionado. She has taught workshops on topics that range from getting organized, to digital scrapbooking, to writing for the media. She has promoted and managed a range of community events from Children's Day activities to a week of family events.

Nikki has a diploma in Freelance Journalism, and a diploma in Internet Marketing and E-Commerce. She was a part time Public Affairs and Media Specialist for almost 20 years and had many articles published in magazines and newspapers.

CPSIA information can be obtained at www.ICGtesting.com
Printed in the USA
LVOW040510140512

281525LV00028B/8/P

9 780987 255303